AQA Express Arts

GCSE

Trudi Dyer
Bernard Fallon
Anette Stücker
June Williams
Keith Woolfenden

Series editors

Bernard Fallon
June Williams

Nelson Thornes

Published in 2009 by:
Nelson Thornes Ltd
Delta Place
27 Bath Road
CHELTENHAM
GL53 7TH
United Kingdom

09 10 11 12 13 / 10 9 8 7 6 5 4 3 2 1

A catalogue record for this book is available from the British Library

ISBN: 978-1-4085-0551-9

Cover photograph by iStockphoto
Illustrations by Rupert Besley and Angela Knowles
Page make-up by Ellipsis Book Limited, Glasgow
Printed and bound in Spain by GraphyCems

Acknowledgements

The authors and publishers wish to thank the following for permission to use copyright material:

Photograph acknowledgements: Expressive Arts Introduction A Alamy/Janine Wiedel Photolibrary and Alamy/Sébastien Baussais, **C** Alamy/Mike Booth, **D** Alamy/Jack Carey; **Chapter 1 opener** iStockphoto; **Chapter 1 introduction** Corbis/Michael Brennan; **1.1A** Rex/Tim Stewart, **1.1B** Jenny Bowers; **1.2A** Fotolia; **1.3A** Bridgeman Art Library/Private Collection/©Succession Picasso/DACS 2009; **1.4A** Bridgeman Art Library/Southampton City Art Gallery/©The Estate of L. S. Lowry, 2009, **1.4B** iStockphoto, **1.4C** M. C. Escher's Möbius Strip II © 2009 The M. C. Escher Company-Holland. All rights reserved. www.mcescher.com; **1.5A** iStockphoto; **1.7A** Corbis/Bettmann; **1.10A** Corbis/Tom Stewart; **1.12D** Alamy/Moodboard; **Chapter 2 opener** Fotolia, **Chapter 2 Introduction A** Simon Drew, **B** Simon Drew, **C** www.cartoonstock.com; **2.1C** The Kobal Collection/Tiger Aspect Pics/Giles Keyte, **2.1D** Maggie Clunie; **2.3A** Reproduced by kind permission of Bishop's College, Gloucester; **2.3A, B, C, D** BBC Motion Gallery; **2.4A, B** BBC Motion Gallery; **2.5A** The Chalk Face Project Limited; **2.6B, C, D,** and **F** with thanks to the students from Cove School who attended the 2008 Screen Academy Summer School, photographs by Keith Woolfenden. Reproduced by permission from Philip Peel of the Bournemouth Arts Institute; **2.7A** Fotolia; **2.8A, B** Reproduced by permission of The Random House Group Limited; **2.9A** Alamy/© Succession Picasso/DACS 2009; **2.9B** Getty Images/Scott Barbour; **2.10A** Fotolia, **2.10B** The Bridgeman Art Library/MAK (Austrian Museum of Applied Arts) Vienna, Austria, **2.10C** Wikipedia; **2.11A** Getty Images, **2.11D** Getty Images, **2.11E** Jazz Badgers; **2.12C** M. C. Escher's Relativity © 2009. The M. C. Escher Company-Holland. All rights reserved. www.mcescher.com; **Chapter 2 closer** Lebrect Photo Library; **Chapter 3 opener** iStockphoto, **3.1A** Getty Images, **3.1B** Anthony Crickmay; **3.2A** Getty Images, **3.2C** Bridgeman Art Library; **3.3A** Mark Balmer, **3.3B** Keith Woolfenden, **3.3C** Faces in the Smoke – The Story of Josef Perl by Arthur C Benjamin Published by Sylvia Perl, 2001. Copyright Sylvia Perl; **3.3D, E** photographs by Keith Woolfenden; **3.4A** Corbis/Alexander Burkatovski, **3.4C** iStockphoto; **3.5A** Getty Images, **3.5B** iStockphoto; **3.6A** Sacred Destinations; **Chapter 3 closer** Wikipedia; **Chapter 4 opener** iStockphoto; **Chapter 4 introduction A (L–R)** iStockphoto, iStockphoto, Alamy/Christine Osbourne Pictures, Alamy/Jon Arnold Images Ltd; **4.2A** Corbis/© The Gallery Collection; **4.3A(i)** Alamy/Lord Price Collection, **A(ii)** Getty Images, **4.3B** Advertising Archives, **4.3C** Westmill Foods; **Chapter 4 closer** Corbis/George Obremski and Corbis/Charles Lenars; **Chapter 5 opener** im Kinsky Kunst Auktionen GmbH; **5.1A** Corbis/Francis G Mayer, **5.1B** Anthony Crickmay; **5.2A** im Kinsky Kunst Auktionen GmbH; **5.3A** Rex Features/Everett Collection, **5.3B** Aardman; **Chapter 5 closer** Aardman; **Chapter 6 opener** iStockphoto; **6.1Ai** Flickr/Kyle Eermoed, **6.1Aii** Alamy/Peter Scholey, **6.1Aiii** Corbis/WWD/Condé Nast, **6.1B** Lebrect Photo Library, **6.1C** Photolibrary/View Pictures, **6.1D** Rex Features/Sipa Press, **6.1E** Alamy/BL Images Ltd; **6.2A** Hawaiian Paradise Trading Company Ltd, **6.2B** iStockphoto; **6.3A** Jess Tice, Fullbrook School Photography, **6.3B** Aaron Law, Fullbrook School Photography.

Text acknowledgements: p33 'The breakdown in family life that threatens us all' by Richard Morrison, The Times, November 7, 2006; p48 'Prayer Before Birth' from Collected Poems by Louis MacNeice, published by Faber and Faber. Reproduced by kind permission from David Higham Associates; p49 'Him Not Grow Up' from Gabriela Mistral Selected Poems by Gabriela Mistral, translated from the Spanish by Ursula LeGuin, published by University of New Mexico Press, 2003; p68 'A beggar smiled at me' from Rumi, Worlds and Paradise, by Mevlana Rumi, selected and translated by Raficq Abdulla, published by Frances Lincoln Ltd; p72 'The words of Josef Perl, a Holocaust survivor', Faces in the Smoke – The Story of Josef Perl by Arthur C. Benjamin, published by Sylvia Perl, 2001.

Every effort has been made to contact the copyright holders and we apologise if any have been overlooked. Should copyright have been unwittingly infringed in this book, the owners should contact the publishers, who will make the corrections at reprint.

Contents

Nelson Thornes has worked in partnership with AQA to make sure that this book offers you the best possible support for your GCSE course. All the content has been approved by the senior examining team at AQA, so you can be sure that it gives you just what you need when you are preparing for your exams.

▇ How to use this book

This book covers everything you need for your course.

Learning Objectives

At the beginning of each section or topic you'll find a list of Learning Objectives based on the requirements of the specification, so you can make sure you are covering everything you need to know for the exam.

Key terms

These words are coloured blue in the text book and their definition will appear in the glossary at the back of this book.

AQA Examiner's tips

Don't forget to look at the AQA Examiner's tips throughout the book to help you with your study and prepare for your exam.

Controlled Assessment tasks

The Controlled Assessment tasks in this book are designed to help you prepare for the tasks your teacher will give you. The tasks in this book are not designed to test you formally and you can not use them as your own Controlled Assessment task for AQA. Your teacher will not be able to give you as much help with your task as we have given you with the tasks within this book.

Visit **www.nelsonthornes.com/aqagcse** for more information.

> **Objectives**
> **Objectives**
> **Objectives**
> **Objectives**
> First objective.
> Second objective.

> **AQA Examiner's tip**
> Don't forget to look at the AQA Examiner's tips throughout the book to help you with your study and prepare for your exam.

AQA GCSE Expressive Arts

◼ Introduction

This book is written to support AQA GCSE Expressive Arts and to guide you through the course. It will explain what you are required to do and how you can produce the evidence to succeed. Most importantly, it will give you the confidence to explore the art forms in combination and enjoy the freedom to work with the language of the arts.

You will be guided towards what makes a good presentation or performance using a range of art form combinations chosen from Dance, Drama, Moving Images, Music, Original Writing and Visual Arts. The chapters will introduce and give you starting points relating to Contemporary Issues and Wider Perspectives. They will guide you to create practical presentations or performances relating to the challenges set, working either alone or in groups. You will find specific arts vocabulary explained in the Glossary on pages 107–8 and examiners' hints to support your work.

The book will emphasise the freedom you have to respond in your own unique and creative way. You can explore the common languages, conventions and traditions shared by the arts and develop an understanding of how the arts complement and support each other. You will be directed towards the understanding of your audience so that you can set out a clear aim for your work.

If you enjoy responding to challenges and finding a way to communicate your interpretation, thoughts and ideas imaginatively to an audience, you will enjoy working with the contents of this book.

Expressive Arts is a 'you can do' course because you can:

- develop your skills in more than one art form
- choose the two or more art forms you will use
- respond using your own ideas
- work either alone or in a group
- present or perform your work
- study existing arts works that will interest and inform you
- use new technologies in your creative work
- use creative writing skills because original writing is an art form
- work with contemporary art forms as they are evolving
- use notes, sketches, photos, diagrams and blogging instead of essay writing
- use continuous writing if you prefer.

AQA GCSE Expressive Arts gives you the freedom to creatively explore and this book will ensure that, as you do so, you are meeting the requirements of the examination.

■ What is Expressive Arts?

Expressive Arts is a 'you can do' examination

If you are interested in studying and developing your skills in *more than one art form* to examination level, in Expressive Arts you can.

You are required to combine *at least two* art forms in every piece of work that you do.

The art forms include Original Writing, allowing you to use creative writing skills learned in English. So if you like writing poetry or prose, you can.

If you prefer to do creative work in a group, you can.

If you prefer to work alone, you can.

If you like doing creative work with video and digital cameras, computers, music composition programmes and new technologies, you can.

Eighty per cent of the marks are awarded for practical work. So if you like to earn your marks by doing practical work in the arts, you can.

No essay writing is needed for the other 20 per cent of the marks either. You are encouraged to use notes, sketches, photos, diagrams and blogging instead. However, if you prefer to use continuous writing, you can.

If you want to learn about the 'big picture' of the arts as preparation for a more in-depth study later at an advanced level, you can.

If you are allowed at your centre to take a single arts subject at the same time as Expressive Arts, you can.

If you want to make connections with the other subjects that you are studying, you can. The contexts of Expressive Arts, contemporary culture and issues, past times and other cultures make this possible.

It may not be possible to do all of the above at your centre; it will depend upon what specialist teachers and what resources are available.

You should always listen to the guidance and advice of your teachers *before* you make any choices. They are likely to know your strengths and weaknesses best.

What you have to do

Throughout the course at your school, academy or college (your centre) you will study and develop techniques and skills in two or more art forms.

The Expressive Arts specification defines six art forms to choose from.

- Dance – any style of dance or genre of movement.
- Drama – any devised or improvised performance or the performance of an original script.
- Moving Images – any sequence of moving images produced by a video camera, digital still camera or other electronic media.
- Music – any genre of musical expression recorded or performed live using an instrument, voice or electronic media.
- Original Writing – any writing in the form of poetry or prose, including play scripts and screenplays.
- Visual Arts – any original image or artefact in two or three dimensions.

Group work and original work

In Expressive Arts you can work on your own or in a small group in any art form/s.

All work in any art form must be original work that is both *created* and *performed/presented*.

Only original work created by you and your group can be assessed.

You can include some existing work in your presentation/performance but only if it forms a small part of a largely original piece.

Throughout the course you will not only be learning to work in two or more art forms you will also be exploring and developing ways in which they can be effectively *combined* in a presentation or performance.

A *Creation is a key part of Expressive Arts*

Assessment tasks

or the Expressive Arts
xamination you must complete
hree assessment tasks. You must
ombine at least two of the
sted art forms in each task.

wo tasks will be set and
narked by your teachers and
ubmitted to AQA as Controlled
ssessment. The third task
vill be set (in the Examination
resentation Paper) and marked
y AQA examiners as your
xamination Presentation.

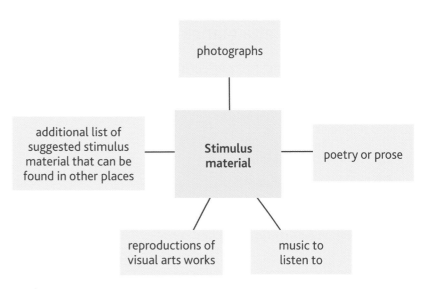

B   *Stimulus material*

reas of Study

ach assessment task must be
et in the context of a *different*
rea of Study. The Expressive
rts specification provides a
amework of *four* Areas of Study
), for examination purposes, you
ill be assessed in three of the
ur Areas of Study.

he Contemporary Issues Area
f Study (D) task is compulsory
nd must be completed as part of
ontrolled Assessment.

ontemporary Issues are
ersonal, social, political
nd environmental world or
ommunity issues that find
xpression through the arts.

C   *Students working on a group presentation*

ou must complete two Wider Perspectives tasks:

   one as part of Controlled Assessment
   one as your Examination Presentation.

Vider Perspectives are:

From Past to Present: developments over past eras; historical contexts.

Peoples and Places: different cultures and traditions; geographical
   contexts.

Universal Themes: themes that, across time and place and world
   societies and cultures, have inspired work in the arts and design.

■ Specification at a glance

Controlled Assessment (60 per cent)

Two assessment tasks, set and marked by your teachers.

1 Contemporary Issues (compulsory) (30 per cent)
2 One task chosen from Wider Perspectives (30 per cent):

   A **From Past to Present**

   B **Peoples and Places**

   C **Universal Themes.**

Examination Presentation (40 per cent)

One assessment task, externally set and marked by AQA, chosen from Wider Perspectives:

   A **From Past to Present**

   B **Peoples and Places**

   C **Universal Themes.**

You cannot submit two assessment tasks from the same Area of Study.

The assessment task that you choose to do from Wider Perspectives for your Examination Presentation must be different from the one you choose to submit for Controlled Assessment. If, for example, you choose to do an assessment task in the context of B (Peoples and Places) for Controlled Assessment, then the task you choose to do for your Examination Presentation cannot be B but it can be either A (From Past to Present) or C (Universal Themes).

Examination Presentation Paper

Three Wider Perspectives Areas of Study questions:

   A **From Past to Present**

   B **Peoples and Places**

   C **Universal Themes.**

You will be able to choose from two – the two that you have not submitted for Controlled Assessment.

D *A warm up, preparing for practical work*

1 Introducing the Expressive Arts specification

Area of Study D: Contemporary Issues

Contemporary Issues is an Area of Study and one of two assessment tasks that must be completed for Controlled Assessment. It is worth 30 per cent of the total examination marks.

All Controlled Assessment tasks:

- will take about 50 hours to complete
- will be carried out with the guidance and supervision of a teacher.

Contemporary Issues is a *compulsory* Area of Study – so there is no choice, everyone has to do it.

What is a contemporary issue?

It is important to consider both words in the title, **contemporary** and **issue**.

'Contemporary' means belonging to the world as we live in it now, whether it is our home or school community, the society of our own country or a society in another part of the world. So, part of this task is to develop an understanding of what is happening in contemporary society. You may do this in other subjects as well.

An 'issue' is an important subject for discussion. Issues frequently feature in the news and usually focus on something that is going wrong. People will have different views about how to put it right and may even consider that there is nothing wrong anyway. So part of this task is to understand more about an issue by gathering information about it, to make up your own mind about it and to express a point of view about it. You will probably do this in other subjects as well.

Expressive Arts differs from other subjects in that you are studying:

- contemporary issues *as expressed through the arts*
- how a point of view can be expressed in an arts work through the language of the arts
- how arts works can influence an audience by asking them to think and make up their minds about an issue.

In this task you will be expressing your ideas about a contemporary issue through your chosen art forms.

A Kim Phuc, made famous as a survivor of a napalm attack in the Vietnam War

1.1 Contemporary Issues tasks

▪ What you have to do for a Controlled Assessment task

All Controlled Assessment tasks are divided into three parts:

- Preliminary Studies (5 per cent of the total examination marks).
- Practical Portfolio (15 per cent of the total examination marks).
- Presentation/Performance (10 per cent of the total examination marks).

Your teacher will give you a suitable Contemporary Issues topic (see page 20) and two existing arts works to study that relate to the topic.

Your studies of two existing arts works is the Preliminary Studies part of the task (for more guidance see pages 21–2).

Then, either on your own or in a group you will:

- choose a starting point for your practical work from your studies
- develop your ideas through practical exploration
- carry out preparation work ready for a presentation or performance
- write evaluative comments about your work as it progresses.

Evidence of this development work and evaluation comments are submitted in a Practical Portfolio.

Throughout this book, for each practical activity, there are instructions about what should go into the Practical Portfolio.

Your Presentation or Performance is the third part of the task.

A *Banksy graffiti art – a good example of a Contemporary Issues arts work*

Activity

1 Photo **A** shows Banksy's 'Big Brother' graffiti art on a wall near Oxford Circus in London. It is asking its audience to think and make up its mind about the 'Big Brother' issue. The presence of the graffiti art is itself an issue for local residents. Carry out the following steps to analyse Photo **A**:

a   Photocopy or scan the photo, and cut and paste it in the centre of a page.

b   Then, making notes around the illustration by writing or typing into text boxes, list the four component images that make up the picture and explain what you think they are communicating.

c   Say who you would expect the intended audience to be.

▪ What a Contemporary Issues presentation or performance must have

Photo **B** combines a simply stated but eye-catching colour drawing of a wind farm looking very 'at home' in a beautiful landscape, with words which make a punchy statement to provoke thought. Its title gives it extra punch by referring to a well-known protest song from the 1960s.

Dylan was right.

The answer is blowin' in the wind.

There is an energy debate about to happen.

The powers that be think the answer is nuclear power.

It's even being called the environmental choice by some.

It's good to see the art of spin is still alive and kickin'.

Of course, we think the answer is to consume less.

And yup, we are all part of that problem.

And therefore, all part of that solution too.

But at the same time we need to invest in renewable energies.

To harness the wind, the sun, the waves, to develop biomass fuels etc.

Yup, the technology needs to be worked on to make it more efficient. But so does the desire to do so.

So before we get railroaded into building more nuclear power stations, can anyone tell me what we are going to do with the waste from the last ones?

B   *An illustration by Jenny Bowers from an eco-friendly clothing catalogue*

The statement presents an issue: Is the nuclear option the 'greenest' way to generate electricity for the future? The statement argues strongly *for* developing wind-generated renewable energy and *against* the nuclear option.

Photo **B** has four elements:

- it is based on an issue
- it expresses a point of view about the issue
- it is intended to influence its audience by asking the audience to think and make up their mind
- it combines two Expressive Arts art forms – Visual Arts and Original Writing.

The final presentation or performance of an Expressive Arts task in Contemporary Issues *must have the same four elements* as the Jenny Bowers illustration.

The style and content of the piece will also be determined by the audience you choose, so it is important to decide on your **target audience** in your early planning. *You are required to state what your target audience is.*

In Chapter 2 of this book there are lots of examples of Contemporary Issues arts works for you to study and practical activities for you to try.

Activities

Look carefully at all of the elements within the study material (Photo **B**) and search for possible starting points for practical work on the issue of renewable energy.

Decide what point of view you want to express, choose *three* of the art forms from the list, then jot down answers to these questions:

2   What would you use as your starting point for each art form?

a   Original writing   b   Music

c   Dance   d   Moving Images

e   Visual Arts   f   Drama.

3   Which other art forms would you combine with each art form?

4   How would the finished piece be presented – as a live performance, as a recording, in an exhibition, etc.?

5   Who would you choose to be your target audience?

1.2 Some Contemporary Issues topics

Poverty

- The poverty that can be found in inner-city estates and the associated problems of violence, crime, illness and poor educational opportunities.
- The causes of poverty in third-world countries – unfair government, factional warfare, famine.
- Rescuing poor, orphaned children through adoption.

Global warming

- Individuals reducing their carbon footprint – changing modes of transport.
- Dealing with weather disasters – flooding, drought, hurricanes, bushfires.

The changing family

- Children coping with parents changing partners.
- Single-parent families.
- Gay couples – civil partnerships.
- Arranged marriages.
- Marriages of mixed race/religion.

Renewable energy

- Wind farms.
- Hydro-electricity.
- Harnessing wave power.
- Solar panels.
- Geothermal.

Bullying and harassment

- At school.
- In the family.
- In relationships.
- In the workplace.

A *A wind farm*

Gangs, alcohol abuse, knives and guns

- Young people hanging out in gangs.
- Violence and drug habits.
- The links between alcohol abuse and antisocial behaviour.

1.3   Introducing the Wider Perspectives

Wider Perspectives Areas of Study

For the examination you must complete *two* assessment tasks from Wider Perspectives Areas of Study, one for Controlled Assessment and one for the Examination Presentation. The two tasks must be from *different* Areas of Study.

There are three Wider Perspectives Areas of Study:

- **From Past to Present:** developments over past eras; historical contexts.
- **Peoples and Places:** different cultures and traditions; geographical contexts.
- **Universal Themes:** themes which, across time and place and world societies and cultures, have inspired work in the arts and design.

A Wider Perspectives task *must have a different artistic intention and a different target audience* to the Contemporary Issues task.

Objectives

Find out about Wider Perspectives Areas of Study.

Find out how a Wider Perspectives task differs from a Contemporary Issues task.

The Wider Perspectives Controlled Assessment task

As with the Contemporary Issues task, all Controlled Assessment tasks are divided into three parts:

- Preliminary Studies (5 per cent of the total examination marks).
- Practical Portfolio (15 per cent of the total examination marks).
- Presentation/Performance (10 per cent of the total examination marks).

All Controlled Assessment tasks:

- will take about 50 hours to complete
- will be carried out with the guidance and supervision of a teacher.

A   Picador *by Pablo Picasso*

When you do a Wider Perspectives task as a Controlled Assessment task, your teacher will give you a suitable topic and two existing arts works to study that relate to the topic. Photo **A** gives an example of an existing art work.

Your studies of two existing arts works is the Preliminary Studies part of the task.

Then, either on your own or in a group, you will:

- choose a starting point for your practical work from your studies
- develop your ideas through practical exploration
- carry out preparation work ready for a presentation or performance
- write evaluative comments about your work as it progresses.

Evidence of this development work and evaluative comments are submitted in a Practical Portfolio. Your presentation or performance is the third part of the task.

Wider Perspectives tasks vary between the three examination categories outlined earlier. Below are examples that have been used previously. You can use them as inspiration for your Expressive Arts course.

Some examples of From Past to Present (A) topics

- Pantomime – its origins and popular seasonal appeal.
- The connections between the blues and the growth of jazz and popular music.
- The 1960s era – the music, the fashions, the social developments.
- The poetry of the World Wars and the Irish 'Troubles'.
- Women in society – the Suffragette Movement in the past and 'girl power' in the present.
- Pilgrimage – Chaucer, medieval Christian pilgrimage; the Annual Hajj, modern Muslim pilgrimage.
- Enslavement – the slave trade of Afro-European past, child labour in the modern developing world.
- Fashion design in historical periods and in modern times.
- The development of film and television genres.
- Industrial and technological revolutions.

You may have come across some of these topics in History, English Literature and other arts subjects.

A The Canal Bridge *by L.S. Lowry*

Activity

1 Look carefully at all of the elements within Photo **A** and search for possible starting points for practical work that contrasts the energies, patterns and rhythms of work and play.

a What would you use as your starting point for a piece combining Music and three-dimensional Visual Arts?

b What form would the finished piece take?

c What target audience would you choose?

Some examples of Peoples and Places (B) topics

- Inuit art and culture – for example, carvings of sea life.
- Turkish art and culture – for example, carpet design.
- Chinese art and culture – for example, animated dragons used in ceremonies, dragon myths, terracotta warriors.
- Native North American art and culture – for example, mask design.

- Japanese art and culture – for example, paintings of mountains and the sea.
- Australian aboriginal arts and culture – for example, dream-time images.
- Indian art and culture – for example, dance styles, representations of myths.
- The artwork in places of worship of different world religions.
- Arts works inspired by nature – for example, English Romantic poets such as Keats or Wordsworth.

Activity

2 Look carefully at all of the elements within Photo **B** and search for possible starting points for practical work which could express your imaginative ideas about magic happenings or destruction caused by a Chinese dragon.

a What would you use as your starting point for a piece combining Original Writing and Dance?

b What form would the finished piece take?

c What target audience would you choose?

B *Chinese dragon with reflection*

Some examples of Universal Themes (C) topics

Universal Themes are themes that occur and recur in the arts and decoration of different times and different cultures – for example:

- patterns
- reflections, refractions, shadows
- revelations
- dreams
- the seasons
- earth, air, fire, water
- the planets, time and space travel
- science fiction
- weddings, births, deaths, life after death
- visual illusions.

In Chapters 3, 4 and 5 of this book there are lots of examples of Wider Perspectives arts works for study and practical activities for you to try.

C Möbius Strip II (Red Ants) *by M. C. Escher*

Activity

3 Look carefully at all of the elements within Photo **C** and search for possible starting points for practical work which could express your ideas about a cycle of events from which there is no escape.

a What would you use as your starting point for a piece combining Drama and two-dimensional Visual Arts?

b What form would the finished piece take?

c What target audience would you choose?

1.5 Wider Perspectives Examination Presentation task

An Examination Presentation task is divided into two parts:

- Working Processes (20 per cent of the total examination marks).
- Final Presentation (20 per cent of the total examination marks).

You will be given an Examination Presentation paper with three questions. Each question provides stimulus material for one of the three Wider Perspectives Areas of Study. Photo **A** is an example of the stimulus material you may get.

You will have completed and submitted one piece of work on a Wider Perspectives Area of Study. You cannot do the question on that same Area of Study, so that leaves two questions for you to choose from.

Your teacher can help you to choose and understand the questions and will give you time to investigate the stimulus material and plan your work. At the end of this preliminary preparation period you will be given 15 hours in which to complete your practical work. To make sure that the examination is fair for all candidates, teachers will supervise what students are doing at all times and verify that it is entirely their own unaided work.

On your own or in a group, you will use the stimulus material as a starting point for your work. You will then develop your ideas through practical exploration and carry out preparation work ready for a presentation or performance. Your preparation and development work must be recorded in your Working Processes submission (for guidance see page 104).

Your Final Presentation (or Performance) is the second part of the task.

A *Hot air balloons over water*

1.6   From a study to a presentation

In the following chapters you will see how a study of arts works begins the journey of developing ideas, acquiring skills and structuring the material generated. Through a working method of improvising/exploring, responding, rehearsing/developing and managing time, you will move with confidence towards presenting/performing the work to an audience.

A study of arts works

- Critically analysing and understanding contextual influences.
- Communicating knowledge, understanding and connections between the arts works studied.
- Understanding how the language of the arts is used to express ideas about the topic.

Developing ideas

- Responding to the study material and identifying a starting point and ideas to explore.
- Thinking about the imaginative and the innovative and communicating with flair.
- Acquiring the confidence to experiment and explore the collaborative language of the arts and challenging yourself to achieve.

Structuring

- Deciding on the aim of the piece, the art form combinations and the target audience.
- Organising the chosen elements into an original, sophisticated structure.
- Understanding the importance of structure in shaping work in an innovative way.

Acquiring skills

- Practical exploration and experimentation with specific skills in both of your chosen art forms.
- Identifying and developing skills, processes and techniques to realise your creative intentions.
- Using skills and techniques with accuracy and control.

Working method

- Responding, improvising, reviewing, modifying and refining.
- Rehearsing with consistent attention to detail, managing your time effectively and working well in a group.
- Using chosen skills, techniques and compositional elements effectively.
- Analysing, evaluating and providing the evidence trail.

Presenting

- Knowing what makes a good performance/presentation that communicates to the audience.
- Understanding how to prepare to communicate your ideas.
- Applying knowledge and understanding of how the art forms relate and interact with each other in your presentation.

1.7 A study of arts works

You will start your journey in Preliminary Studies where you will investigate existing arts works. Through your study you will:

- come to understand how the arts communicate through a specific style
- analyse the **construction** and form of the works
- learn about the skills and techniques used in the works
- discover the artist's or practitioner's intention and the influences that informed the work
- understand and become familiar with the language of the arts.

Through this **study** you will be able to develop a vocabulary and identify elements that you can use in your own original work.

The language of the arts is constantly evolving and progressing, like new words that are added to our spoken language (representing the 'now' of that time). By using elements of the style of the work studied, mixed with your personal interpretation, you can bring an original and innovative contribution to the language of the arts. Experiment with and explore the arts, and aim to use your own unique interpretation in your work.

Objectives

Establish a working method in Expressive Arts beginning with a study of arts works.

Use the Universal Theme of 'a journey' (on the Orient Express) to explore elements of the process.

■ 'A journey' on the *Orient Express*

You will be given two arts works to study relating to the *Orient Express*. Firstly, find out about this famous train that was the inspiration for the Agatha Christie novel *Murder on the Orient Express*. The arts works could be chosen from posters, paintings, books or films that evidence the elegance of the 1930s – the heyday of an *Orient Express* journey – travelling in comfort and style; dressing for dinner; being thoroughly spoiled; good food, music and friends. Your teacher will give you guidance to help you with your study so that you can communicate knowledge and understanding of the arts works. You will also need to make connections between them and understand the contextual influences.

You could expand your study material and listen to 'The Little Train of the Caipira' from *Bachianas Brasileiras No. 2* by the Brazilian composer Villa-Lobos. The journey on this train is a complete contrast to the opulence of the *Orient Express*.

A *The Orient Express*

Activities

1. Find an image, a piece of text or a short extract of film about the *Orient Express* and study what you have resourced. Working on your own, choose words that you associate with the stimulus material. Share these words with your group. Discuss the similarities and differences. This activity will help you to analyse and understand how images, film or text can tell you more than just the basic facts about the *Orient Express*.

2. Create a **soundscape** to represent the mood and atmosphere of travelling on the *Orient Express*.

   Use only your voice and sounds that you can make from objects around you.

   Guidance

   Do not be too serious about this exercise – let it be fun and possibly a little silly as you experiment with and explore the language of sounds. The simplest of sounds used with imagination and creative flair can successfully engage an audience and transport them back in time to a journey on the *Orient Express*.

3. To move towards a creative and expressive response, ask yourself and the group these questions:

   a. What are the key **signifiers** of this style of travel?

   b. What are the people on the train wearing?

   c. What are the distinctive qualities of their speaking voices?

   d. What are the physical indicators of style and confidence?

   e. What style of music is in the background?

Hint

To generate your own IDEAS to work with

Investigate the study material and your exploration will lead you to:

Develop ideas that will enable you to use the material.

Explain your train of thought in your Practical Portfolio.

Analyse by breaking it down into its component images.

Select those that are best suited to achieving your aim.

Moving on to practical development work on the topic 'a journey'

you are able to answer the questions asked in the activities above en brilliant, you are on your way. You may not be able to answer em, or perhaps you do not like the topic, you have no ideas and u think soundscape was 'rubbish'. This is not such a bad thing. The mous composer and lyricist Stephen Sondheim said, 'Art isn't easy' d it is not, but it can be fun. With guidance from your teacher find other arts work that relates to the topic 'a journey' and that you d your group find more inspiring. By finding a way forward you are king ownership of the task and this will help you to develop ideas for ur own unique arts work. This course is flexible enough to allow you do this, but always consult with your teacher first.

eliminary Studies

r each task you will analyse the images, style, form and construction arts works and find out about their historical, cultural, social and litical contexts using notes, diagrams, sketches, etc. This evidence st be submitted for Controlled Assessment in your Preliminary dies. Your teacher will give you detailed guidance about how this is be organised but it must cover:

analysis of arts work one and arts work two

explanation of the connections between them.

1.8 Developing ideas

This is the stage when you will be exploring ideas to develop into your own original presentation or performance.

If you are working alone you may find it helpful to share your ideas with others to get their feedback.

It is important that you:

- establish what good group work is
- understand the collaborative language of the arts and understand how to progress your ideas using a framework
- think about the imaginative and the innovative and experiment with the rich language of the arts, creating work that is unique.

If you are working in a group this may well be the most challenging part of the working process, although it is also important to recognise that there are challenges of working alone too (e.g. not having anyone to discuss ideas with).

Positive group work is essential so that all of the group members feel that they have ownership of the development of ideas. There will be a range of personalities in your group – for example, those who are assertive, those who like their own ideas and others who will be mediators. Some will not have the confidence to share their ideas with the other group members.

■ 'Know your group' activity

Identify which type of group member you are from those listed below and use this information as a positive way forward to inform your working method:

- Confident and full of ideas.
- Lots of ideas but lacking the confidence to share them.
- A bit distracted by other things at the moment.
- Happy to work with your own ideas or those of any of the other group members.
- A natural leader, good at negotiating a way forward.

All but one of the above points can be positive attributes if you manage them sensitively. If you are easily distracted, now is a good time for you to realise that this is not productive in any process and the fact that you do not contribute may cost you marks.

If you are the confident group member, encourage those who lack the confidence to share their ideas. Use the natural leader in the group to organise a schedule of work that you can all contribute to, ensuring that you meet deadlines. Work as a team, all contribute and all agree the ideas to develop.

Good group work is about listening to others, sharing ideas and agreeing the material that is chosen to develop. Everyone in the group should contribute to the working method.

A Pull your weight and share the loa

The collaborative language of the arts

xpressive Arts requires you to work with *two art forms*, that are totally tegrated. Think of weaving them together in such a way that they omplement and support each other. This allows you to create rich, xpressive and colourful language, and to communicate in a way that different from the discrete art forms.

he art forms are:

- Dance
- Moving Images
- Original Writing
- Drama
- Music
- Visual Arts.

ome examples are as follows:

- Film making and production skills (Moving Images) are combined with acting (Drama), the writing of a screenplay (Original Writing) and design aspects, e.g. costume design and making (Visual Arts).
- Performance dance combines choreography and dancing (Dance) with creating accompanying sound (Music) and costume/mask/set design and construction (Visual Arts).
- Song writing combines writing lyrics (Original Writing) with composing (Music).
- An exhibition where two- or three-dimensional Visual Arts may be integrated with a piece of music composed specifically to be played as the sequence of images are viewed. A mobile may be created using the words of an original poem (Original Writing) combined with shapes and structures (Visual Arts) that give added meaning to the poem.
- A children's story (Original Writing) with original illustrations (Visual Arts).
- A music composition (Music) presented in a CD case with original cover design (Visual Arts).

Activity

How to find creative and imaginative ways to combine art forms

Here are five group members with their chosen art forms. The task they have been given is to create a presentation using the theme 'a journey' (use the Orient Express ideas generated on page 20). Organise this imaginary group so that they may all contribute to the presentation.

If these art forms do not represent those that your centre will be using, ask your teacher to assign more appropriate art forms to the fictitious group members. You may also need to modify the character profiles.

Share your ideas with other groups and, with the help of your teacher, rate your ideas against 'The imaginative, the innovative and communicating with flair'.

Group member A:
Music and Drama. A great singer, very confident.

Group member B:
Visual Arts and Drama. Excellent drawing skills with quirky ideas.

Group member C:
Music and Original Writing. Talented pianist, thoughtful lyricist but passive.

Group member D:
Drama and Original Writing. Very organised, good at bringing ideas together.

Group member E:
Moving Images and Dance. Good at research and loves old black-and-white films.

1.9 Acquiring skills

Across the six possible art forms there are too many techniques to list here, so ask your teacher to help you compile a list for your chosen art forms and to relate these to arts works that you have studied. Accuracy and control are also important in your application of techniques, so spend some time thinking about how you will show accuracy and control.

Objectives

Develop your skill in a range of techniques in both of your chosen art forms.

Apply these techniques with accuracy and control in order to realise your creative intentions.

Activity

What is a technique?

Below are some definitions. Discuss these in your group and with your teacher. Choose one that you feel best suits what you understand *technique* to be.

- A special ability in an art form that is acquired through training.
- A method, procedure, knack or trick of doing something well.
- A proficiency or refinement applied in an artistic context.
- An aptitude and competency particular to a specific task.
- A practical method applied to a particular presentation.

AQA Examiner's tip

In Expressive Arts it is very important to develop your technique skills and apply them in the context of both art forms.

Towards the end of Developing Ideas (page 23) you were thinking about the imaginative and the innovative, and beginning to experiment with the rich language of the combined arts so that you can communicate with flair.

Innovation is a challenging requirement of Expressive Arts because it is often quite difficult to introduce something new, different and perhaps unexpected. Challenge yourself with the topic 'a journey'. Perhaps think of a modern application of the theme, e.g. 'the gap year', 'voluntary service overseas', or 'travelling in unexpected style because you have been upgraded at the airport'. This always brings a smile to everyone's face. Flair and imagination is what follows as you work with your innovative ideas.

A *Upgrade, brilliant! No challenges about that*

1.10 Structuring

Through **structure** you will be able to give shape to your work.

Successful structures engage the audience by:

- keeping the content short and concise
- refining the work through careful editing
- having varied content and pace.

Objectives

Understand the importance of organising the ideas you have generated using structure.

Temporal structure

To fully experience written and performance art **forms** the audience normally starts at the beginning and stays with the piece, experiencing the sequence of changing events until the end is reached. This is temporal structure.

In your composition include only what is essential to communicate to an audience. Keep the content minimal, leave out non-essential 'clutter' and provide visual variety.

Spatial structure

Where the audience is free to 'read' a painting or sculpture in the way they wish. Paintings and drawings are defined by their frame or edge as they fill a two-dimensional space, whereas sculpture and architecture exist in a three-dimensional space.

Combining temporal and spatial structures

Moving Images (where the piece is basically a film) will have a temporal structure because it has a narrative with a beginning, middle and end, and a two-dimensional spatial structure applied to the framing of each camera shot.

Drama and Dance also have a temporal structure but they are performed in a three-dimensional space, so the shaping and placing of performers has a three-dimensional spatial structure.

A *Using levels in performance presentation*

Arrange these imaginary sections of work in such a way that they communicate to the audience that working as a team is productive.

A Five performers enter and occupy the performance space. Each is present as an individual and they do not relate to each other as they travel their chosen route in this short section of work.

B Two musicians sing a short eight-bar extract, one after the other (part of a short original solo song about isolation). Two music promoters enter (Drama) and approach each individual musician. A third character enters (the choreographer) and puts the two musicians together. The two short melodies are now performed together. The two original promoters exit from opposite sides.

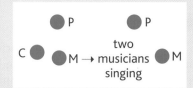

C Five performers enter and present the original song about isolation but sing as one, in the style of a girl/boy band; a confident and secure team performance.

D Five performers in the performance space, a trio and a duet. At the end the trio split the duet up. The duet exit from opposite sides.

E Two duets, one dance and one drama. A soloist sings. The duets perform and freeze to allow the audience to hear and see the dance and drama. The singing continues throughout as accompaniment (original short song about loneliness), the singer is always present on stage.

There are several ways of doing this:

A → E → A → D → A → B → A → C

or E → A → D → B → C

Any section can be repeated if you wish.

By analysing how you have chosen to organise the imaginary sections you will find that there are many possible ways of bringing work together to suit the aim of the piece. Members of your group will each share their different solutions. Some will use an existing organisational pattern and others may use a unique structure specific to the needs of this imaginary performance.

Structures to investigate are:

■ **episodic** ■ **contrapuntal** ■ **sequential** ■ **collage**.

1.11 A way of working

■ Working method

Your working method is your **strategy** for organising and managing all of the contributing parts of this examination. Devising your working method will involve:

- identifying and understanding the parts of the examination so that you allocate time for each of them
- productive use of the preparation time you have available
- avoiding **the Mugwumps!** This is not another technical term, it is a made-up, expressive word for the times when nothing seems right.

The aim

This is a clear and simple statement, written in your Practical Portfolio, of the intention of the presentation or performance. For example: The aim of my performance is to communicate to my target audience, through music and drama, the luxurious style of travel enjoyed by the passengers on the *Orient Express* in the 1930s.

The target audience

The chosen audience will inform you of the best style of communication. Their anticipated age, how well they understand the arts, and the location of the performance or presentation will all provide reasons for devising your work in a specific way. Keep notes of your thoughts and decisions about this in your Practical Portfolio.

The two chosen art forms

There may be more than two art forms working together in your performance or presentation, but you must nominate the two that you personally wish to be marked on. As you devise your work aim to use both art forms through a balanced range of techniques.

Responding

After your studies of the arts works chosen, you will respond to what you have learned and experienced. Your response will give you ideas that can be progressed in your practical work.

Improvising

This is a spontaneous response to an idea or stimulus material. To improvise or explore you need to feel secure with your group so that you can take risks with your chosen art forms and, through this exploration, develop a vocabulary of ideas that you may or may not use in your work.

A *The Mugwumps versus strategy*

Reviewing

This is when you, on your own or with a group, look at all the ideas you have generated and consider those that are best suited to bring together for your performance or presentation. At this stage you will identify any additional techniques that you will need to develop to allow you to achieve your creative intentions. Keep a record of this, including evaluative comments, in your Practical Portfolio.

Rehearsing or developing

After reviewing your experiments and improvisations you will begin the rehearsal/development process. Aim to rehearse or develop your work with consistent attention to detail. Rehearsing or developing is when you will apply your skills and techniques in a chosen context, relating to your aim and considering your target audience. Rehearsing and developing needs careful planning. Keep a record of your progress and write evaluative comments in your Practical Portfolio.

Refining

This is an ongoing activity that involves making decisions about what stays in and what is removed. Set aside regular rehearsal/development time to monitor the progress of your work. Ask yourself questions: does this section work? If not, why not? Can you (or you and your group) see a way of improving what you have done or will it have to be edited? Creative flair sometimes encourages complication. Courage is needed to edit the material and carefully remove unnecessary parts. This will benefit the whole piece. Write evaluative comments about your decisions in your Practical Portfolio.

Performing or presenting

This is the best part of this course. If you have worked well and/or as a team and produced your very best work, it will give you pleasure to share this with your target audience. A dress rehearsal or preview for your friends is good preparation to check that you are communicating your aim and it gives you one last opportunity to refine. A dress rehearsal or preview is also the last opportunity to write evaluative comments.

Practical Portfolio

This is the essential collection of material that provides the evidence of your work as it progresses, e.g. a log or blog and notes, diagrams and sketches. You will build up your Practical Portfolio alongside your practical work and your teacher will guide you about how it is to be organised (see pages 31–2 for further information).

Evaluative comments

These are comments that you make about your work and that of others at all stages of the creative process, and they are included in your Practical Portfolio. An evaluative comment should be short, factual and clear, telling the reader what you did and why you did it. It will say why it worked or was not successful, providing an alternative for the least successful parts (see page 32 for further information).

AQA Examiner's tip

Write regular evaluative comments in your notes. Evaluative comments show how well you have understood the study of arts works, the working method of ideas and the communication using the language of the arts in your performance or presentation.

Activities

Final task

Take the ideas you generated for the 'a journey' activity (see page 23) and give them an annotation (A, A1, B, etc.).

Check that all of the ideas are included and combine any of them that fall into obvious groupings.

In your group discuss the following question and record your decisions.

1. What is the aim of your piece?

2. Who are your target audience?

3. Negotiate and agree the most suitable way of organising your ideas (there will be many ways of bringing the ideas together but one will probably suit the visual imagery in most of your group's minds).

4. How will you begin and end?

5. Check that each group member has the chance to show their best work through their best art form combination.

6. Check that you are all challenging yourselves to create an innovative performance/presentation that integrates the chosen art forms in an imaginative way.

1.12   Presenting

Depending on your choice of art forms you will either perform or present your work.

You are encouraged to present your completed practical work to an audience. This could be:

- an exhibition of your work
- a screening of the work
- a live performance.

A   Engaging your audience

A performance implies a two-way process – you the presenter/performer communicating to your audience and the audience receiving this. For this work you must **engage** your audience. If the audience is not focusing on the performance or presentation you will not be communicating.

Presentation/performance

You will communicate your ideas through your chosen art forms.

You will apply your knowledge and understanding of how your chosen art forms relate to and interact with each other.

You will use relevant techniques and compositional elements to realise your creative intentions.

If you are working in a group you will be assessed on your individual contribution.

B   Would you be happy to be the performance?

C *Dealing with hecklers*

Understanding your audience

Stand-up comedians learn to deal with hecklers just as theatre actors had to – investigate Nell Gwyn and the restoration theatre audiences. We should perhaps be grateful for the modern audience who are polite and well behaved. Your audiences of parents and friends are the most forgiving of recipients.

- Do not patronise your audience. Tease them a little, draw them in and then take them on a journey with you. Give them moments of security.
- It is important to have a strong performance presence, the confidence that comes from thorough rehearsal and the security that comes from good team work.
- Do not be afraid to challenge your audience if the performance requires this.

D *A Visual Arts piece engaging its audience*

1

Conclusion

You now have a working method to guide you as you explore your chosen art forms. Build up your own vocabulary of style and techniques. The emphasis in this course is on you creating original presentations/performances, not on you creating a **pastiche** of existing work.

As well as submitting Preliminary Studies, you must keep a Practical Portfolio. This will provide evidence (which will be assessed) of the progress of your ideas and practical work from your chosen starting point through to the completed presentation or performance. It will also provide evaluative reflections of your work in relation to the work of others at all stages of the development of the piece. If you are working in a group, you and everyone in the group must keep their own Practical Portfolio and, although you will often refer to other members of the group, your Practical Portfolio must track *your contribution* to the piece as it develops. It must be a record of *your work*. There must also be evidence of your progress in the two art forms you have chosen to work in.

What does a Practical Portfolio look like?

The format of a Practical Portfolio is not specified. Your teacher will give you instructions about how it should be put together in your centre. There is no given size. All of the following points are general guidelines:

- Performance students: keep a log that is supported by photographs, video clips and short experimental sound recordings.
- Visual and written art forms will keep early and developmental sketches and drafts. It is probably easiest to keep all of this on a computer, including photographed or scanned sketches if you wish. If you are able to do this in your centre, make sure that all your work is safely backed up. If it is lost it cannot be marked.
- Where appropriate, diagrams, storyboards, plot outlines, mind maps and cut-and-paste layouts are all encouraged and acceptable. Any developmental recordings must not exceed five minutes playing time.
- You can use a sketch-book, notebook or folder to document all of this evidence.

In every case the aim should be to keep the portfolio as small as possible. It would be foolish to leave out anything that is important evidence, but it would be equally foolish to leave in material that is not useful evidence (because it is not helpful to a teacher or moderator who has to wade through your work and mark it).

Throughout this book guidance is given regarding what should go in the Practical Portfolio for each practical activity.

You must provide evidence in ways which are appropriate to the two art forms that you are working in.

Smart portfolio

Evaluative comments

In your Practical Portfolio you need to include evaluative comments which must:

✔ show how elements of the studies are influencing your developing work.

✔ analyse and evaluate the effectiveness of your own work in relation to the work of others. What did I do? Why did I do it? What theory supports this? How well did it work?

Checklists

The material in your Practical Portfolio to support your practical work should provide evidence of:

✔ the aim of the piece and the intended audience for the presentation/performance

✔ how elements of the arts works studied are influencing your work

✔ how your ideas relate to the chosen starting point

✔ how you are shaping and structuring your ideas as your work progresses

✔ how you have explored and experimented with processes and techniques in each of your two chosen art forms

✔ the modifications and refinements that you make

✔ how you apply and combine your chosen art forms to communicate your aims.

The evaluative comments that you write should provide an analysis and evaluation of your work at all stages and should comment upon:

✔ the reason for the choices that you make, such as your intended audience and the elements you choose from other work

✔ the decisions you make relating to the shaping and structuring of the piece and to modifications and refinements.

✔ the processes and techniques you choose to use and how they relate to the aims of the presentation

✔ the strengths and weaknesses of your work

✔ the effectiveness of the presentation in achieving your artistic intentions and communicating to your chosen audience.

2 The family

Explore the issue of the family through each of the art forms.

Understand how the language of the arts can be used to communicate and raise the audience awareness of issues relating to family life.

Studying a Contemporary Issue in detail: 'the family'

Teenagers are often quite wrongly blamed for issues relating to the breakdown of family life. Photo **A** is a humorous look at the stereotypical, know-it-all teenager. It is good to have the right to reply and redress any family imbalance. In Expressive Arts you can do this.

In this chapter you will begin to discover how, through your presentations and performances, you can share with the audience a balanced view of issues that relate to family life.

As you will see from the article below, nothing changes!

The breakdown in family life that threatens us all

> *I am in shock. I have just read two books that expose Britain's teenagers as vicious, lawless, contemptuous of authority, alienated from family and society, fixated on drugs, drink, crime and lethal weapons, and wrapped up in a gang culture that leads nowhere except incarceration or an early grave.*
>
> *Yes, the youth of 1938, when Graham Greene wrote* Brighton Rock, *must have been a ghastly lot. Surpassed, perhaps, only by the young thugs of 1962, as portrayed in Anthony Burgess's* A Clockwork Orange *– though the author said that he based that novel's most violent scene on a horrific attack on his wife in the 1940s.*

Richard Morrison, *The Times*, 7 November 2006

A *Yeah but, home is sweet*

B *Rules are made to be broken*

C *Family life*

The family explored through Dance

Art-form combinations

You should be aware of the fifteen possible art-form combinations arising from the six art forms that are available to work within the Expressive Arts course.

In your group consider the possible art-form combinations that are available to you in your particular centre. There may be a choice – within your group you will need to consider how you can communicate your ideas through the combined arts that you have identified.

Using the vocabulary wall in Diagram **B** identify the words that relate to your two art forms. These words are explained in the following chapter and you will find study materials and activities to help you explore the language of the arts.

Objectives

Be aware of the fifteen possible art-form combinations arising from the six art forms you can work with.

Investigate aspects of the film *Billy Elliot* and develop ideas from it.

Use the film as a starting point to create a short dance.

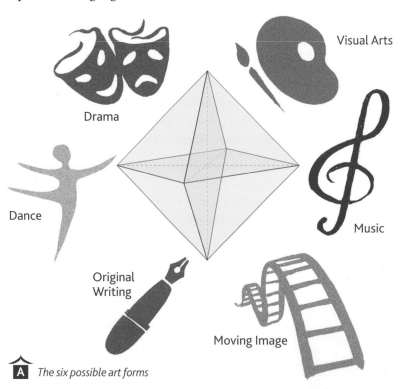

A *The six possible art forms*

Drama
Visual Arts
Dance
Music
Original Writing
Moving Image

character	dynamic	atmosphere
pace	symbolism	
space	situation	timbre
continuity	structure	
expression	phrase	monologue
rhythm	composition	
harmony	relationship	expression
mood	flashback	
soliloquy	genre	flow
shape	style	
sequencing	melody	action
narrative	tempo	

B *Vocabulary wall*

Study material

The film *Billy Elliot* is set in 1984 in a mining town in northern England. The miners are on strike, money is tight and the atmosphere is tense. Eleven-year-old Billy Elliot lives with his father and brother – who are participating in the strike – and his grandmother. Billy does not like the boxing lessons that his father encourages him to take. Instead, he prefers watching girls' ballet classes and joins in. When his father finds out about Billy's secret passion for dance, Billy is in trouble. But with the support of his ballet teacher, Mrs Wilkinson, Billy continues training and manages to secure an audition for the Royal Ballet School. Now he has to open his heart to his family.

Activities

1   Find five words from the word wall that relate to a chosen art form.

2   Find another five words that relate to different art form.

3   Identify those words that relate to several art forms.

4   Find out the meaning of any words that are new to you.

This film provides some excellent starting points from which to explore ideas about Billy within his family, through the art form of Dance. You can analyse any aspect of the film, but the following three sequences are distinctive because they show Billy dancing for various reasons:

- 'I Like to Boogie' shows the joy that Billy gets from dancing.
- 'Dancer of Defiance' shows Billy dancing to impress his father.
- The audition shows how his love for ballet has developed.

Starting points for ideas

Choose one of the three scenes listed, then look at the dance content within the scene and identify the movement material. Is it all one particular genre of dance (e.g. ballet) or are aspects from other genres of dance included? What effect does that have on an audience?

Now ask yourself how this particular scene has inspired you. What ideas has it given you to create the following?

- The storyline for a dance.
- Characters for a dance.
- Steps for a dance.

Make a record of all of your ideas.

C   *Billy Elliot*

Developing your ideas

In developing your ideas you can start by reproducing the movement material seen in the film. Then to make it your own and exciting for an audience you should aim to be adventurous in your choice of dance movements. It is important to create several **motifs** that communicate your intentions of the dance.

Once you have created several motifs, use **choreographic devices** to help you create the dance. Repetition is a good device, but if over-used too much it makes a dance predictable, so developing your ideas by changing direction, speed or level is a start. If you are in a group you also need to consider the way you use formations. Everything done in a straight line lacks depth, so consider working on diagonal lines.

If you are unsure about the dance terminology used, ask your teacher to explain it further.

Once you have created your dance it needs to be practised so it can be performed with confidence and accuracy. A performance should show a lot of energy, use space really well and communicate your ideas clearly to an audience.

AQA Examiner's tip

- Start by **improvising** movement ideas based on what you want your dance to be about. Do not stick with the first few ideas but explore further to get the best possible movement material for your dance.
- When you are creating the parts of your dance you need to consider your audience constantly and what you want them to see.
- Make sure you practise your dance in the intended performance space. Ask someone to watch you and give feedback on your performance.

D *Using asymmetry and the diagonal to add variety to choreography*

Integrating Dance with other art forms

Now explore how to integrate your dance with another art form. Here are some suggestions.

Dance and Drama: think of your dance as a dream sequence and use it within a piece of drama to look back at an event that occurred in the past.

Dance and Original Writing: create a piece of original writing, such as a poem based on Billy growing up without his mother. You could record the poem and use it as the soundtrack for your dance.

Dance and Music: using music software or an instrument that you play, compose your own music to accompany your choreography. Use the music you compose to help you express the mood of your dance.

2.2   Dance vocabulary

Having completed the introductory task you should now be able to put the Dance terms in Diagram A into the appropriate boxes in Table B. They are a range of terms used to show the physical skill of a dancer such as walking; the interpretative skill of a dancer such as the use of focus; the choreographic devices used in a dance such as repetition and the way a dance is formed through a structure like a duet. Some of these terms have been explained previously, but if you are unsure about a particular term, try and look it up on the internet or ask your Dance teacher what it means.

genre   following the leader   space   walk   levels   jumps
shape of space   timing   parting   pathways   stretch
stepping   action   rhythm   speed   size of movement
motif development   bend   run   turn   fall   travel
transitions   twist   direction   mood   question and answer
transference of weight   motif   balance   unison   expression
relationships   focus   phrasing   gesture   middle and end
style   stillness   technique   expression   duet   climax
canon   logical development   dynamics   focal point
energy   beginning   contrast   repetition   rondo   mirroring   motif
space   unity   focus

A   *Terms that can be applied to Dance*

B   *Skill boxes*

Performance skills	Choreographic skills
focus	unison
Dance skills (action content)	**Form of dance**
walk	duet

Activities

1   Draw a copy of Table **B**. Some of the terms have already been included.

2   Sort out the words in Diagram **A** into the categories identifed in your table.

3   Put the sorted words into the appropriate skills box. When you've finished, compare your answers with a partner.

Appreciation skills

In order for us to understand a dance we need appreciation skills such as:

- **Solution to a problem** – how did you decide what to do for your dance, was it a group decision or your own?
- **Statement of theme** – if your dance was based on 'I like to Boogie', how did you show that Dance can be a lot of fun?
- **Original and appropriate movement** – how did you select your movement material and how did you make sure it was original?
- **Unity of structure** – was your dance put together randomly or did you try and follow a structure (e.g. beginning, middle and end)?
- **Content (idea)** – what movements or motifs did you create to show your idea?
- **Rhythmic interest** – was your dance based on the same rhythmic pattern or did you try and vary it to make it more interesting?
- **Spatial interest** – how did you use space? Were you planning your formations and did you make sure they changed during the dance?
- **Use of dynamics** – this is the way you perform movement, soft or forceful for example. Did you vary this within your dance?
- **Relationship to accompaniment** – did you use the music and follow every beat or did you try and express the mood of the music?
- **Performance quality** – how well did you use expression in your dance?

Activity

4 Now check how many skills you have used for the dance that you created using the *Billy Elliot* stimulus. List all of the skills you have used.

Extension activity

Ask yourself the questions posed in the appreciation skills list and explain how the questions could help you to find out if the dance you have created is successful.

Definitions

Space

- General space is where the body moves. You can use little space (moving in a small circle) or a large amount of space (travelling).
- Personal space is the space immediately around one person.

Action

- Refers to the movements you are able to perform such as gesture, travel, turn, jumps, stillness, balance, bend, stretch, twist, stepping.

Relationship

- There are various different relationships. They can refer to people or objects that you are moving with, e.g. are you dancing a solo dance (on your own) or are you dancing with one (duet) or two (trio) other people or within a larger group? Are you using a prop, e.g. dancing with a coat on, or using an umbrella or a chair?

Mood

- Not all dances tell a story, some evoke moods. In Dance, mood often relates to a prevailing atmosphere or feeling. For example, the mood in the introductory dance in *Ghost Dances* (choreographed by Christopher Bruce) is scary, whereas the mood in 'I like to Boogie' in *Billy Elliot* is very happy.

Expression

- This is a performance skill, it is the way you communicate your dance idea to the audience, e.g. you are showing loneliness and wrap your arms around your body. The way you do this by using rhythm, speed and dynamics helps the audience understand your purpose.

2.3   Using Drama techniques as an exploration tool

Exploration improvisations

Improvised 'off text' Drama techniques, usually used to discover more about a scripted play, can also be used to explore the characters and situations in any narrative. This section provides an opportunity for you to use the 'swapping characters' and 'outcast' techniques to explore a television play that deals with family issues.

A   *Students going through a final check before the performance*

A 'cutting-edge' television play

When we look at the grainy pictures on pages 40–2 it is difficult to believe that *Cathy Come Home* was ever 'cutting-edge' television, but in 1966 it was. It merged drama and documentary with the aim of raising public awareness of the social issues of homelessness, unemployment and the right of parents to keep their own children; issues not thought about much at that time. '4,000 children are separated from their parents and taken into care each year because their parents are homeless', is the message displayed before the credits at the end of the film.

The play tells the story of Cathy and Reg, a young couple who start married life full of optimism. Finding that they cannot afford to bring up their children or rent a home of their own, their story plunges through a series of misfortunes. With nowhere to live they find themselves at the mercy of the authorities who treat them like criminals and they are moved into separate hostels, which causes their marriage to break down. Cathy and her children eventually end up sleeping rough on a bench at a train station; soon after officials forcibly take the children away from her.

There are several sequences that could be explored using improvisations. We will explore two heart-rending sequences, one near the beginning and one at the end of the play:

■ the eviction (see Photo **A** and Activities 1–3)
■ when the children are taken away (see Photo **B** and Activity 4).

Eviction sequence in more detail

■ Reg piles up furniture to make a barricade and boards up doors and windows.
■ Photo **A**: Cathy and the children are terrified as they watch the door and their barricade being battered down by bailiffs.
■ Photo **B**: the bailiffs (the figures to the left and right of the frame) succeed in forcing an entry.
■ Reg angrily threatens a bailiff and is pulled away.
■ The bailiffs remove the furniture and stack it in the street watched by a crowd of nosey neighbours.

A *Eviction sequence. Cathy and Reg cannot pay the rent …*

B *… and are forcibly evicted with their children*

Activities

Use the 'swapping characters' technique to explore the characters and the situation in the eviction sequence.

1 In a group, improvise the sequence with the main characters – you can imagine the children and crowd outside.

2 Repeat it three times with everyone swapping characters each time.

3 In a group discussion consider:
a which interpretation of each character was the most convincing
b which version of the situation was the most convincing and why.

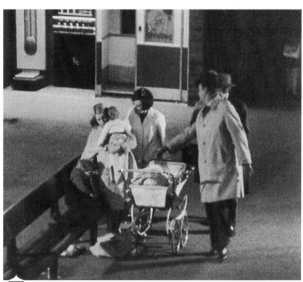

C | *Cathy has lost everything and is homeless*

D | *Four officials find Cathy and take her children away*

Outcast

'Outcast' is an improvisation technique which explores the **motivation** that drives the actions of people caught up in an incident where someone is the victim of 'anti' attitudes such as prejudice or bullying.

1   Arrange your group in the performance space with everyone at the edge facing one person in the middle. Those at the edge represent the 'anti' attitudes of people. The person in the middle represents the feelings of the outcast.

2   Everyone at the edge must think of a short threatening, patronising or sarcastic statement that sums up an 'anti' attitude towards the outcast. Repeat the statements in a simmering quiet way and direct them at the outcast.

3   Continue chanting the statements in a louder more aggressive way, moving a step or two closer to the outcast and taking up a position with an appropriate gesture. Repeat this several times until a tight circle surrounds the outcast. Each time the chanting can get louder and blur together, and the postures can become more threatening – but there should be no physical contact and it should stop if the outcast can't cope.

4   The performer playing the outcast must respond spontaneously to this negative energy directed at them, probably becoming more and more humiliated and sinking to the ground in a defensive posture.

5   Repeat the whole activity with someone different being the outcast each time and then share your thoughts about what you thought and felt when performing the outcast and the other roles.

Activity

4   Explore Photos **C** and **D** using the 'outcast' technique. Cathy is the outcast and the officials are the 'anties' who think she is a failure because she is an unfit mother and she is homeless.

Hint

Evidence in the Practical Portfolio

Ask someone to take some photographs of your group doing **exploration improvisations**. Paste them into your log or blog and give them captions to explain what is happening.

While the experience is fresh in your memory take a few moments to jot down in note form what you found out about the characters, their motivation and the situation. You could link these notes to the photographs.

2.4 Drama theatrical devices: vocabulary and use

Real-time sequencing

Drama can tell a story (narrative drama) and it can be acted in a way that is as real as possible (mirror-of-reality drama) with the scenes arranged in the normal time sequence, starting at the beginning and finishing at the end.

Activities

1. In your group, study the caravan sequence from *Cathy Come Home* by reading the script or watching the DVD. Start from where Cathy and Reg arrive at the caravan site and finish where they have to sell the caravan.

2. Make a list of the other characters, apart from Cathy and Reg, that are needed and decide who is going to play them.

3. Improvise the sequence, repeating each scene to get it right before moving on to the next.

Although disappointed at first, Cathy and Reg settle happily into caravan life with its simple, basic routines, and they get on well with the other caravan dwellers. Their contentment is shattered when the caravans are maliciously set on fire and destroyed.

Parallel action

Narrative drama may have two or more stories (sub-plots) that run parallel (parallel action) and then merge. Cutting from one story to the other is a device which adds interest to drama by breaking up the real-time sequence.

Activity

4. There is a scene in which the residents of a new housing development nearby have a meeting to decide how to get rid of the 'slum on wheels'. In your group, create a 'family' from the new estate – there could be parents who support the removal of the caravan site and a child whose best friend is one of Cathy's children. Develop a sub-plot that climaxes with the attack on the site when caravans are stoned and burnt.

A *The beginning …*

B *… and the end of the caravan sequence*

Shuffle sequencing

Begin a story somewhere in the middle – a moment of particularly heightened dramatic action perhaps, something that will have maximum impact on the audience – then flashback to an earlier scene of the story, then fast-forward to a later scene. Continue to shuffle the sequence of scenes to keep the audience 'on their toes'. To help the audience follow the shuffled time sequence, end each scene with a freeze-frame and include obvious clues in what the characters say in the dialogue, that indicate the point they are at in the sequence of events. You could also use a narrator who steps out of the action and speaks directly to the audience and then steps back in as a character. The performance space could be divided and two or more scenes, which occur simultaneously in time, could be performed using action cross-fades and silent animation.

Stylised drama

Drama presentations can represent ideas, thoughts and feelings and explore relationships, hopes, fears, problems and issues that are important to us all in abstract ways using stylised drama. Instead of being 'characters', performers can be a 'personification' or character stereotype. Outcast on page 41 is an example of this and could be included in a final performance.

The movement aspects of a theme can be presented in slow motion, or simple actions could be repeated to a rhythm. Movement with repetitions and rhythms can be developed in choreographic ways to become dance-like. Several performers could move in unison; choral movement can communicate in a powerful way.

Instead of just speaking to each other, stylised drama techniques can be used to represent what is going on in characters' heads. Characters can share their thoughts directly with the audience by using an aside, thinking aloud, or a soliloquy or monologue. The audience then feel much more intimately involved. It can get quite exciting if several actors represent different 'voices in the head' and this can lead into a fantasy or dream sequence. Ideas in short statements or significant words can be repeated and become rhythmic. Repetitions and rhythms can be developed and become more like poetry. Several performers could speak in unison; choral speaking can communicate in a powerful way especially when combined with choral movement.

Activities

6   In your group, look at the elements of Outcast on page 41 and develop them by organising and choreographing them, using repetitions and rhythms, into a piece of choral movement and choral speaking. Then take motifs and develop them into dance, music or poetry.

7   In your group, create a voices-in-the-head sequence or a dream sequence for any character or incident from these drama activities. It could be in the head of Cathy in the Outcast exercise above. It could be the voices of conscience, reason, cowardice and bravado in the head of someone from the new estate contemplating violent action. It could be the dreams or nightmares of any of the children in the narratives.

Activity

5   Take the narrative that you created in Activity 1 and add further sub-plots. Keep the focus on issues about the attack on the caravan site. Add friends/neighbours of the parents. They might disagree about whether it is right to take direct action, i.e. about taking the law into their own hands. The child may not be allowed to bring a friend from the caravan site home to tea; they may have to meet in secret. Plan how you could perform your new narrative drama using shuffle sequencing. If you have the time, try it out.

AQA Examiner's tip

- Be concise. Leave out the boring bits of your story; move on to the next interesting bit of action.
- Avoid real-time sequencing. Use as many theatrical devices as you can.
- Develop your piece into dance, music or poetry.

Hint

Evidence in the Practical Portfolio

Ask someone to take some photographs or video clips of your group doing development improvisations. Paste these into your log or blog and give them captions to explain what is going on.

Keep a brief record of the narrative and stylised drama sequences that you create – you could use a storyboard.

In 2002 Christina Aguilera released the song 'I'm OK' on her album *Stripped*. The song tells the story of a young girl's pain at seeing her brutal father regularly beating her mother and how the mother and daughter lived in fear of him.

The girl is recalling events in the past and thinking about how they have influenced the person she has become. She credits her mother for the love that gave her the strength to survive and asks her father if he understands what lasting psychological damage he has done.

Research shows that the abused often become abusers. Look at the image of the man striking the boy while his mother looks on (Photo **A**).

Objectives

Explore the stimulus of the dysfunctional family.

Create a Moving Images presentation, integrating at least one other art form.

Activities

In your group or working alone:

1. Choose a sequence of images invoked by the song and create a storyboard for your video.

2. Show the differences between the past and the present by using **monochrome** for events in the past.

3. This topic could be very emotive for some people. Explore ways of maintaining the impact required without upsetting people. You might experiment with freeze frames or sequences of still photographs.

◯◯ links

Read the song lyrics at this website www.lyrics.com. Search under Christina Aguilera I'm OK.

AQA Examiner's tip

Working to a song or a piece of music gives a finite length to your video and can influence some of the editing decisions.

A *Exploring images and considering their impact*

Is the mother indifferent to what is happening, or is she too afraid to interfere on her son's behalf?

What effect is the man's violent behaviour having on the boy? Does he think that this is normal family behaviour?

What effect do you think the boy's upbringing will have on his own behaviour as he grows up and when he has a family of his own?

Discuss the range of answers to these questions with the whole group and use this to inform a broader response. Refer back to Chapter 1 where good group work is discussed and be sure that the subject matter is not making anyone in the group uncomfortable or stopping anyone from participating.

Activity

4   Through improvisation, explore the relationship between the boy and his mother.

Create a video diary which explores the situation from the boy's perspective. You could write a script of the boy's innermost thoughts and combine this with flashbacks of the events that he is describing.

Integration

Using the information gained through your research, create a video presentation entitled 'Vicious circles', exploring how the abused often become abusers themselves.

You might combine your acting with hard facts, presented either as part of the script or as overlaid graphics.

You can integrate your Moving Images work with other art forms.

Drama: using improvisation, create characters based on your research and place your characters in scenes that you will film and then edit.

Original Writing: present the hard facts gained during your research as part of a script. This script may be used by the actors to give the camera a precise schedule for the running order of the chosen shots. Or you could be making use of a narrator to progress your work.

Visual Arts: present the information in a visual way by creating graphs, pie charts, etc, or you could design and present a visual representation of a challenging situation. Using **chroma-key** techniques real characters could then interact with original drawings.

You will need to be creative in your choice of shots and in your editing skills. Think about the film maker's use of music to help create the atmosphere of the presentation.

You may have someone in your group who can compose original music for the atmosphere. As with film music, the timing will need to be very accurate.

Try to ensure that your Moving Images presentation, whilst being emotional and atmospheric, is also factually accurate. You are raising awareness of a sensitive situation and, in some cases, you are educating your audience.

Hint

Type the name of your editing software, followed by 'free tutorials', into Google for a selection of free tutorials which will help you to develop your creative editing skills.

2.6 Moving Images vocabulary

If you are interested in exploring the idea of presenting your work in the form of a video or DVD production, you will need to be familiar with the basic language and working practices of film and television.

- **Accuracy**: in a video context this means the care with which you follow the shooting script and set up your shots. This same care and attention to detail also needs to be evident in your editing. Remember, although each frame of video represents only 1/25th of a second, even one frame in the wrong place will be noticed by the viewer.
- **Pace**: the speed at which the programme moves forward. Pace is affected by the length of each shot, the selection of cuts or transitions and by the choice of music.
- **Structure**: the framework of your programme, as demonstrated by your storyboard – a clear beginning, middle and end.
- **Composition**: the arrangement of subjects within a shot and the placing of shots within a programme.
- **Flow**: the way in which your sequence of images conveys your ideas to the viewer, helping to create atmosphere.
- **Continuity**: ensuring that scenery, costume and the actors' positions are correct throughout the production.

Objectives

Understand a range of Moving images vocabulary.

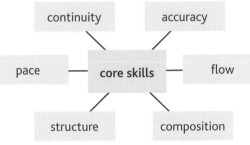

A Core skills for creating a good Moving Images presentation

B Year 10 students working at the 2008 Screen Academy Summer School

> Moving Images are defined as the original creation of sequences of moving images produced by video cameras, digital still cameras and/or electronic media.

AQA Expressive Arts GCSE Specification

links

The following book will give you more information and help you to develop your skills in the exciting world of video making:

Chris Patmore, *Get Started in Short Filmmaking*, Methuen Drama 2005

The process of making a video programme

The process of making a video programme can be split into three sections:

Pre-production

This is the planning and preparation phase in which you will research your material, choose your locations, write your script, decide upon your camera shots and draw your **storyboard** and **shooting script**.

Ensure you have a variety of **types of shot**, starting with an establishing shot and then showing detail with medium shots and close-ups.

Production

This is the shooting of the programme. For this phase you will need some basic equipment including a **camcorder**, a tripod, at least one fully charged battery, and of course a means of recording your work such as a video tape, a DVD or a memory card. You might also need an additional microphone and a pair of headphones for monitoring the audio.

It is vital that all of your shots are in **focus** and that you follow the shooting script, paying particular attention to continuity.

Post-production

This is the editing phase. Contrary to what many people think, this is not just an opportunity to cut out all of the mistakes – it is a very important part of the creative process. You can connect your camcorder to a computer and, using an editing package such as Windows Movie Maker, Adobe Premiere Pro or Avid Media Composer, you can capture and edit your video footage. Experimenting with **cuts**, **transitions** and special effects will help add pace and interest to your programme. You can easily add **graphics** and **audio dub** speech and music into your production to help create a suitable atmosphere.

C   *A pre-production storyboard*

D   *Production: Year 10 student working with professional actors at the 2008 Screen Academy Summer School*

E   *Post-production: Year 10 student working on an Avid Media Composer edit suite at the 2008 Screen Academy Summer School*

Original writing can take many forms. Below are two poems set out in different styles. Read through them and then move on to the activities.

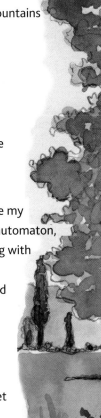

Prayer Before Birth

I am not yet born; rehearse me
In the parts I must play and the cues I must take when
　old men lecture me, bureaucrats hector me, mountains
　　frown at me, lovers laugh at me, the white
　　　waves call me to folly and the desert calls
　　　　me to doom and the beggar refuses
　　　　　my gift and my children curse me.

I am not yet born; O hear me,
Let not the man who is beast or who thinks he
　is God come near me.

I am not yet born; O fill me
With strength against those who would freeze my
　humanity, would dragoon me into a lethal automaton,
　　would make me a cog in a machine, a thing with
　　　one face, a thing, and against all those
　　　　who would dissipate my entirety, would
　　　　　blow me like thistledown hither and
　　　　　　thither or hither and thither
　　　　　　　like water held in the
　　　　　　　　hands would spill me.

Let them not make me a stone and let
　them not spill me.
Otherwise kill me.

by Louis MacNeice

Activities

1　Consider the shape of both poems and then make notes about:

a　The ways in which the shape of each poem might influence how you speak the poem.

b　How the shape could be expressed in a three-dimensional Visual Arts piece.

c　How the shape could be expressed in a Dance motif.

2　Consider the images in both poems and then:

a　Make a list of the images in each poem and select some from each that you particularly like.

b　Make sketches for a composition combining these images in a painting.

c　Make notes about how these images might be expressed in a drama or film scene.

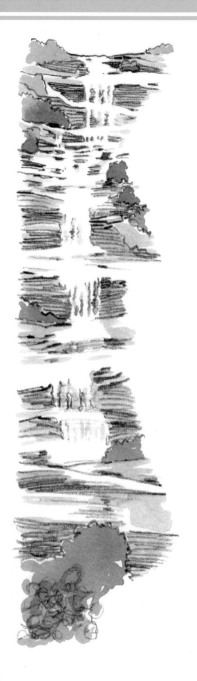

Let Him Not Grow Up

  May my little boy
stay just as he is.
He didn't suck my milk
in order to grow up.
A child's not an oak
or a ceiba tree.
Poplars, meadow grasses,
things like that grow tall.
My little boy
can stay a mallow-flower.

  He has all he needs,
laughter, frowns, skills,
airs and graces.
He doesn't need to grow.

  If he grows they'll all come
winking at him,
worthless women
making him shameless,
or all the big boys
that come by the house.
Let my little boy
see no monsters coming.

by Gabriela Mistral
(translated from the Spanish by Ursula Le Guin)

You will have analysed lots of poems in English Literature lessons and there is little space in this book to go into the understanding of poetry in great detail, so these pages concentrate on just a few elements. Apart from the subject, meaning and ideas expressed in a poem there are three elements of poetry which make links with other art forms: images, shape and rhythm.

Images

Like all works in any art form, a poem is mostly built up of images – words or phrases which stimulate a 'picture' (or sound, smell, sensation or feeling) in the imagination of the reader. Since all art forms make use of images, an image appearing in a poem can easily be transferred and expressed in another art form.

Activity

3 Consider the rhythm in both poems and then:

a Make a note of the key features which make the rhythmic structures different.

b Experiment with music motifs which express these differences.

c Improvise a dance to each poem with just the poem being spoken as the accompaniment.

Shape

The shape of a poem on the page is a part of the way that the poem communicates and it is part of what makes a poem different from prose. There are thin poems and fat poems, depending on the length of the lines. There are tiny poems that seem to be floating in a great sea of space. There are poems arranged in regular blocks down the page. There are poems with each **stanza** (verse) crafted into an interesting shape. Poems come in lots of shapes and sizes. Shape is also a key element in the way that Visual Arts and Dance communicate.

Extension activity

Choose one of the poems that you particularly like and find a copy so that you can appreciate it as a complete poem. You could then develop and apply some of the activities with which you have experimented.

Rhythm

Poetry is always musical. This is another thing that makes it different from prose. The music in a poem is created by the **metrical structure** of the lines, the musical phrasing resulting from the order of the words and length of sentences, and by **rhymes**, **assonance** and **alliteration**. Poetry and Music therefore work well together, and Dance is also dependent upon rhythm and phrasing even if it is unaccompanied.

The poems and Contemporary Issues

Parenting and caring for children are issues that are part of 'the family', and that starts at childbirth. The poems both relate to a period around the time of birth; 'Prayer Before Birth' is pre-natal and 'Let Him Not Grow Up' is post-natal. They are both in the form of a prayer. The first is in the voice of the unborn child and the second is in the voice of the mother, and both raise fears about what life will be like after childhood. The unborn child wants help with those aspects of life which cause humiliation and those which might stifle individuality; the mother wants to be over-protective of her little boy by not allowing him to grow up.

Both are parts of longer poems: 'Prayer Before Birth' is the last four stanzas of an eight-stanza poem and 'Let Him Not Grow Up' is the first three stanzas of a six-stanza poem.

You will see that in 'Prayer Before Birth', stanza 5 (the first in this excerpt) has seven lines and stanza 7 (the third) has 10 lines and that each stanza is one long sentence. This is part of a pattern in the poem. The main stanzas get progressively longer and are arranged in the same way, like a cascade of water flowing down steps, so that stanza 7 almost looks like a triangle and is the largest cascade. 'Let Him Not Grow Up' continues in the same way as these first three stanzas, short lines and short sentences, so the poem looks tall and thin on the page.

A Mother with her baby

2.8   Original Writing vocabulary

There are four types of Original Writing that you are most likely to use in Expressive Arts: poems, stories, play scripts and film scripts.

There is information about the key terms used in poetry and the presentation of poems on pages 48–9.

There is guidance about the presentation and writing of a film script on pages 92–3 in Chapter 5, 'Manisha and the Mystery Christmas Card'.

Here we will consider writing a story and writing a play script.

Objectives

Improve the presentation of stories and play scripts.

Develop some useful writing techniques.

Writing a story

Stories are usually written in the past tense – as if recalling something that has already happened – but apart from that, there are very few rules. The writing of a story gives you lots of freedom. It can be set in the past, present or future; in the real world or a fantasy world; in the thoughts or dreams in someone's head; in any setting, time of day, season or weather conditions. The story can move freely and at will between any of these. It can include speech and can describe action; it can be a story for very young children; it can be a scary science fiction story – indeed it can be anything you want.

To make your story writing successful there are two tips worth considering:

- create the right atmosphere
- use the right vocabulary.

Atmosphere

Describe the setting and conditions in a way which matches and enhances the action and mood of the story – we call this 'atmosphering' the story. So a bleak story should be in a bleak setting and a cosy warm story should be in a cosy warm setting. A gloomy mood should be atmosphered by gloomy weather conditions; a threatening situation by threatening conditions. This will link with Visual Arts if you choose to illustrate your story.

A   The Big Friendly Giant, *by Roald Dahl*

Activity

1   Think of a list of words that could be used to describe atmosphere in a story. Divide them into bleak and cosy settings.

Vocabulary

Choosing the right range of words for your story is very important. There are different vocabularies that you should consider:

Audience: an audience of very young children, for example, can only understand very simple words.

Character: part of establishing a character is to let each character use words in a particular way – the captain of a spaceship giving orders will use a different vocabulary from a little girl bossing her younger brother about.

Specialisms: every area of activity (real or imaginary) has its specialist vocabulary – for example, a story set on a sailing ship must use sailing vocabulary accurately.

Atmosphere: words themselves have an atmosphere, so when atmosphering the story use appropriate words – for example, use scary words to describe threatening conditions.

Genre: different types of story are written in different styles – the difference is usually quite subtle – for example, you would tell a science fiction story in a different way to a ghost story.

Make sure that the vocabulary you are using is appropriate; do some thorough research.

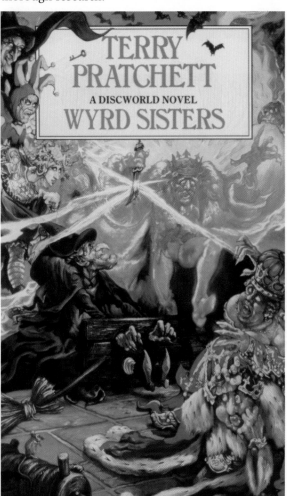

B   *The cover design of* Wyrd Sisters *by Terry Pratchett*

Activities

Story writing and Visual Arts

2. Use Photo **B** as a stimulus for a story. What genre would it be? What would the characters be like? Who are your audience?

3. Look at Photo **A** 'Homecoming by the Winter Wood' on page 92 of Chapter 5. You will see three figures – a man, a woman and a child. Using these as your main characters, and the snow covered woods as the opening setting, write a story which moves to other settings, and then draw sketches to illustrate the other settings that you choose. For each setting, change the atmosphere as much as you can.

Play script writing

4. Write what you think happens next in the sample play script in Photo **C** on page 53. It is in the style of a television 'soap'. Practise formatting the scene to look like the 'Waterside'.

Writing a play script

When writing a play script (or a film script) atmosphere and vocabulary continue to be important. Atmosphering is done by indicating what set, sound and lighting effects (or location and background music) you want at each point in the dialogue. The following example is a suggested template for formatting a play script.

Waterside

Characters:

George Fradley Landlord of the *Duck and Paddle*

Sally Fradley The Landlord's wife

Kayleigh Fradley Their daughter (Kay). A student

Jimmy Maslin Artist. Lives in Weir Cottages

Aileen Drake Jimmy's partner. A middle-aged hippy

Sophie Copping Student. Friend of Kayleigh Fradley

Kevin Parris In computers. Sophie's boyfriend

Skip Retired woman. Lives on the narrowboat *Wanderer*

Scene 1

The scene is set in the Duck and Paddle*, a canalside pub. It is early evening in the winter. There is an old-fashioned bar and there are tables laid out for customers. The whole room is dimly lit.* **Jimmy Maslin** *and* **Aileen Drake** *are sitting at the bar.* **Skip** *is sitting on her own at one of the tables in a corner. There is no one behind the bar.*

Sally Fradley enters behind the bar. Jimmy and Aileen are surprised to see her.

Sally: What the hell are you two at? You look as if you've seen a ghost.

Aileen: Sorry Sally. We thought that you were at the hospital with Kay.

Sally: Yeah, well, I was. She's out of danger and doing all right now. George is still there. My daughter's as tough as old boots, y'know. I was just getting in the way.

Jimmy: Look, Sally. If there's anything we can do …

Kevin bursts in the main door R. with Sophie close behind.

Kevin: (sounding very pleased with himself) This must be the place. Kay said it was next to the canal.

Sophie: (massaging his ego) O, Kevin, you're so clever to find it. I'm sure I couldn't have.

They go to the bar.

Sally: Did you just say Kay? My daughter calls herself Kay. Do you know her?

A loud splash followed by shouting is heard outside.

AQA *Examiner's tip*

A key factor in assessing the success of Original Writing is the ability of the writer to use words which creatively atmosphere the narrative. Another key factor is the ability to use appropriate vocabularies that achieve the aims of the piece.

Hint

Evidence in the Practical Portfolio

Keep early drafts of all original writing to show how it was amended and improved as your work progressed. Write evaluative comments that give reasons for the amendments you make.

Visual Arts and a second art form

The *Family of Saltimbanques*

Pablo Picasso painted *Family of Saltimbanques* in 1905 and he reworked it several times.

At this time Picasso was in a period of his work referred to as Early/Blue Period and he was inspired by his visits to the *Cirque Médrano* in Montmartre. He painted the circus on many occasions between 1904 and 1906 and it may be that he felt a strong association with the avantgarde artistic leanings of circus performers.

Travelling circus performers have a tradition in literature and art. They were often a poor but proud and independent group of performers, and had a strong sense of family.

The figures in Photo **A** stand in a bare, undulating landscape, and although Picasso has brought them together in a balanced composition, each individual appears isolated from the others and from the audience (the viewer). The painting has a thoughtful mood and it may be that Picasso is the Harlequin.

A The Family of Saltimbanques, *Pablo Picasso, 1905*

There is a family **stereotype** in circus. Families generally have a specific area of skill such as tightrope walking, trapeze or equestrian talent. Skills were passed from father to son and mother to daughter. The modern *Cirque du Soleil* still uses family groups in the shows – one show is even called *Saltimbanco*.

Activity

1   Research the importance of circus at the turn of the 20th century. Are there other artistic works that use circus as a stimulus? (See for example Renoir, Toulouse Lautrec, Degas.) What was Paris as a city like at this time?

You could explore the music of the time, the importance of the circus as entertainment and the famous dance company *Ballet Russe*.

links

To learn more about Picasso visit the website of the Picasso Museum at www.museupicasso.bcn.es/en/.

links

Watch the clips from the *La Nouba* show available at: www.youtube.com

Search for: La Nouba High wire

Activity

2   Get some charcoal or pastel and use it to make just five strokes on some paper. Your aim is to represent a family stereotype through these five strokes. Try this activity for at least three family stereotypes.

With practise, you will become quite accomplished at this. Remember, as long as you keep the medium in contact with the paper it counts as one stroke.

The aim is to identify the essential visual elements for the stereotypical image that could be developed into a character.

Bring your images together in grouping. Use your understanding of still images in Drama and Dance to inform your placement of the figures on the page. Share your work with others and evaluate the success of the activity.

Integration

It is important to set aside time to study the naturally occurring links between Visual Arts and the other art forms.

For example: a family group of circus performers at the time Picasso painted *Saltimbanques* would have designed, and had made up for them, a distinctive, durable, colourful and appropriate costume using the fabrics available at that time (Visual Arts). The visual impact of the costume, combined with a dramatic performance entrance, the music and the choreography begins the relationship the performers would have had with the audience. The expectation, excitement and anticipation of the audience were, as they remain to this day, important considerations.

Study the costume designs for the *Cirque du Soleil* highwire acts in both the *Saltimbanco* and *La Nouba* shows. There are clips of both performances on the internet where you can see the visual impact of the costumes in the context of the performance, relating to the set, lighting, live music and drama. The theatricality of the performance is very engaging.

Activities

3   Create a costume design (Visual Arts) for a tightrope walking family act performing around 1900. Write a short extract of script (Original Writing) where the costume design is at the centre of a family disagreement about its suitability in terms of modesty, durability, cost and the established family image.

4   Research the Danish tightrope walker Elvira Madigan. Her life story is very dramatic as depicted in the 1967 film by Bo Widerberg. Mozart's *Andante* from 'Piano Concerto No.21 in C' was used for the film and has become popularly known as 'Theme from Elvira Madigan'. There is also a ballad written by Johan Lindstrom Saxon and a track by the band Komeda called 'Elvira Madigan'.

5   Explore words that visual arts and music share such as colour, contrast, tone and mood. Discuss how you could use music to support the mood and tension in a presentation or performance. Remember: if Music is one of your art forms you must create original music to integrate with your Visual Arts.

Remember

Evidence in the Practical Portfolio

Keep a record of all your starting points for ideas. Evidence supporting your practical explorations is also important, but do not include printouts unless there is detailed annotation on them.

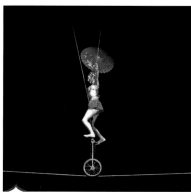

B   Cirque du Soleil, Saltimbanco High wire

AQA   *Examiner's tip*

In your performance or presentation for Contemporary issues, it is important to establish an aim that expresses a point of view.

Extension activity

Using the title 'A fine balancing act' plan out a television documentary about the contemporary issue of modern family life. Develop ideas for the trailer or poster, showing parents trying to balance their work commitment with quality family life. You could use the highwire circus idea and explore set and apparatus design (Visual Arts) in a fanciful, theatrical, kitchen setting and combine this with another art form of your choice.

Core words and their meaning

Colour: the effect on the human eye of light of varying wavelengths creates colours such as red, yellow and blue.

> *Colours, like features, follow the changes of the emotions.*
>
> Pablo Picasso (1881–1973) 'Conversation avec Picasso', Cahiers d'Art, 1935, Paris, vol. 10, no. 10 (translated in Alfred H. Barr Jr, Picasso: Fifty Years of His Art, USA, The Museum of Modern Art, 1946)

A A colour wheel

Composition: the arrangement, placement or design within an art work; where things are placed.

Expression: the artist's feelings, ideas and personality communicated in their art work.

Style: art is organised into different periods and genres such as impressionism, post-modernism and realism.

Mood: the atmosphere in a piece of art, such as John Singer Sargent's *The Sitwell Family*.

Shape: the outward form or outline of something or someone.

Subject matter: what the artist is representing in their art work, such as a person in a portrait.

Symbolism: when something is used to represent something else to give the audience broader understanding.

Almost every culture contains the symbol of the 'Tree of Life', the Earth and the Underworld. Its branches and roots represent a uniting link between heaven, the Earth and the Underworld. Create a Tree of Life using your own ideas and choice of symbols or work in a group to create a collaborative response.

B Tree of Life (Stoclet Frieze), *Gustav Klimt, c.1905*

Activities

Look at the painting *The Sitwell Family* by John Singer Sargent (1900).

Sargent was a fashionable society portrait artist from the late-Victorian and Edwardian eras who was known for the way he captured the charm, elegance and opulence of society at that time. The Sitwell family group poses against carefully chosen heirlooms.

From left to right: Edith the eldest daughter is dressed in red; Sir George the father with hand resting protectively on his daughter's shoulder; Lady Ida, the dutiful elegant wife is arranging flowers; two small sons play contentedly with the dog.

Working in a small group look at the painting and answer the following questions:

C   The Sitwell Family, *John Singer Sargent, 1900 – Rennishaw Hall, Derbyshire*

1   What sort of mood does the painting convey and how does the artist achieve this?

2   How does the composition of the painting capture the status, elegance and opulence of the family?

3   Can you discover the hidden meaning in this painting as the artist is in part communicating an unreal situation? You will need to do some research and find out about Sir George's riding boots and Lady Ida arranging flowers.

Finally, in your group explore possible links to other arts works that can be developed from studying this painting and consider what point of view your group may wish to communicate relating to the Contemporary Issue 'the family'.

Edith Sitwell as an adult became a modernist writer, developed a theatrical image and supported artists in the 1920s. She worked with the composer William Walton in 1922 on an avantgarde combined arts work, called *Façade*. Her nonsensical poetry was performed live, amplified through a megaphone so that it could be heard over Walton's witty music for a small instrumental ensemble. The first performance was called by her brother, Osbert Sitwell 'an entertainment for artists and people of imagination'. The *Façade* poems are studies in onomatopoeia and word rhythms, where the sound of the words is more important than the meaning. Music and language are totally integrated in this rather crazy work. 'Lullaby' and 'Tango' are the most popular tracks. In 1931 Frederick Ashton choreographed the *Ballet Façade* to William Walton's reworked music but without the poetry.

Hardeep Does Family

Hardeep Singh Kohli, a Glaswegian Sikh, is a writer and comedian. *Hardeep Does Family* is the third of a series of programmes for Channel 4. Each programme begins with extracts from Hardeep's stand-up shows. He shares contentious opinions with his audience and then takes these out on the streets to the public. He is not afraid to challenge, with searching questions and sometimes hard-hitting opinions.

Hardeep asks these questions:

- Are families in Britain going down the pan?
- Why have families changed so much over the last few decades?
- Should we aim to reinstate the **nuclear family**?
- Will counselling help to make better parents?

Activities

1. In your groups and before watching the recording of *Hardeep Does Family*, discuss the questions that Hardeep asks.

2. Watch the programme and then return to your groups and revisit the four questions to see if your responses are different.

3. Consider how the programme influenced you or changed your opinion.

Your study of this programme will make you more aware of some young families where teenagers are mums and dads. Hardeep takes on the role of dad for a day to three sons of **absent fathers**. He meets teenage mothers who are bringing up a child alone and a middle-class mum who appears to have it all.

Now that you are aware of some issues relating to modern families, take a little time to think about the many and varied ways that music can contribute to a collaborative Expressive Arts work. Your teacher will guide you towards those that may best suit your exploration of the issue of family life.

Activity

4. Match a music style to these potential characters from the programme:
- the young mother
- the teenage absent father
- Hardeep
- the middle-class mum
- the positive-parenting class leader.

Do this on your own and then share your thoughts with the rest of your group. It must be emphasised that there is no right or wrong matching, just ideas that may work in a chosen context.

Objectives

Explore the language of music through the issue 'the family'.

A   *Hardeep Singh Kohli*

B   *Music styles*

Extension activity

Use any of the ideas in Table **C** and explore them through music. Use a keyboard or the voice to begin with and progress to your chosen instruments.

The core elements of music

hythm, tempo, timbre, melody, harmony and texture are your basic alette – these words are the core elements of music. Think of them s colours that you will use as a basic palette with which to paint your icture in sound.

sing these you will be able to paint your picture with sounds.

ou will structure your elements of music, bringing them together and eveloping them in such a way that supports your chosen meaning. se phrasing, repetition, contrast, dynamics and creative flair to ommunicate your aim to the audience.

AQA Examiner's tip

Composing original music will ensure that it is integral to the collaborative process and complements and supports your other art form.

C *Instrumental music*

Idea	Music
mage of the secure family group	Safe and secure. Melody that is balanced, predictable. Two-bar phrase answered by a two-bar phrase. The melody moves by step and any leaps are to notes of the chords 1 1V or V.
The young mother	Romantic song. The thoughts in a young mother's head although she may be trapped due to the responsibility of parenting.
The absent father	Distinctive, edgy, rhythmic. Free of sentiment, full of life.
Hardeep	A question-and-answer style of phrasing as an introduction, leading to a Hardeep main theme (A). Bold, cheeky, confident, rhythmically secure perhaps with a quirky contrasting section (B).
The class eader	Lyrical, flowing phrase of music followed by a chord progression to communicate the didactic response.

Activity

5 Listen to music that will broaden your understanding of the language of sounds, the weird, whacky and challenging. For example:

- The Magnets: all of their music is created with the voice although some tracks sound instrumental.

- The company STOMP use percussive rhythmic patterns played on familiar everyday items that are not musical instruments. The sounds have an odd timbre due to the unusual sources.

- Minimalist works by Phillip Glass. The six movements of *Glassworks* are short and accessible.

  - Paul Simon's *Graceland* – 'Diamonds on the Soles of Her Shoes'. The track begins with Ladysmith, Black Mambazo singing unaccompanied and is followed by the main song with instrumental accompaniment.

  - The music from the opening of Act 1 of the musical *Sunday in the Park with George* by Stephen Sondheim accompanies the assembly of the set and characters on stage, as the actor who plays the artist Seurat narrates and creates the scene he painted: *A Sunday Afternoon on the Island of La Grande Jatte*. This work links music with set design, lighting and drama.

D *Ladysmith Black Mambazo perform Paul Simon's 'Under African Skies'*

What can you communicate to your audience through music?

- Music can suggest a location and scene before the drama begins.
- Music can enhance the mood and emotion in a presentation.
- Music created for a specific character can announce their presence.
- Song can advance the narrative or consolidate the mood or emotion.
- Music allocated to each character, giving them a separate musical palette of sound, can enhance their distinctive profile to the audience.
- Music can make the listener conscious of a part of the story already exposed.
- Music can enhance the experience and create a dream quality.

Vocabulary

Rhythm: a pattern of sounds.

Tempo: the pace of the music.

Timbre: the tonal quality of the sound that identifies it.

Melody: groups of notes that work together.

Harmony: two or more notes that sound good together.

Dynamics: the contrast and shading of volume from loud to soft.

What you can do with the basic sounds to progress your composition

- Keeping the texture of sound light will allow a heavy moment to punch through when needed.
- Changing the tone quality will give mood and emotion to an identifying melody or motif.
- If you have access to the technology, compressing and filtering sounds can create a special quality of sound for darker moments and scenes that have implications of other worlds or special powers.

E *Students working on a composition*

2.12   Music vocabulary

Using music to set the scene

Music can have an important effect on a performance. It is important to understand the different terms used in creating music. Read through the following pages to familiarise yourself with these terms.

Activities

1   Using keyboards or voice, take a note for a walk using the graphic notation shown in Diagram **A** to guide you. It has three beats in a bar and uses a note, a note above the note, a note below the note and back to the note.

2   Once you have worked out the rhythm, perform this first phrase in a question-and-answer style.

3   The next four bars are a sequence, repeating the first four bars a little higher in pitch. When you can perform this music securely, experiment with the tempo and dynamics.

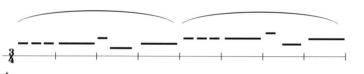

A *Graphic notation to inform activity 1–3*

Activity

4   Use only your voices for melody, and rhythms played on anything in your teaching space. Work in groups of three to five and improvise with your ideas for setting the following scenes through music:

- a wedding
- a military parade
- a game show – the tension before the answer
- the rainforest
- an Olympic medal ceremony
- a birthday party
- a conga.

Extension activity

Look at the example of a graphic notation in Diagram **B**. Can you identify this very famous piece of music?

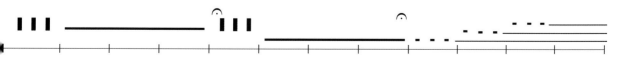

B *Graphic notation for a well-known piece of music*

Vocabulary

Melody: groups of notes that work together.

Rhythm: a pattern of sounds with different combinations of sound lengths and stresses.

Graphic score: a way of notating your musical ideas using symbols, line and pictorial representations to indicate pitch, rhythm and sound quality through short written directions.

Bar: a group of sounds that last the amount of time indicated by the time signature at the beginning of the music. The first beat in the bar is usually stressed. The patterns made by some groups of sounds are given specific names, e.g. Waltz or March.

Dynamics: the contrast and shading of volume.

Phrase: a section of music that has a sense of stability.

Question and answer: two phrases of music that respond to each other and work well, giving a balanced effect.

Sequence: a short phrase of music that is repeated either higher or lower than the original.

Tempo: the pace of the music.

Anacrusic: not starting on the first beat of the bar.

Beat: the regular pulse.

Counterpoint: when two or more melodies play at the same time. They relate and weave together in a horizontal way.

Canon: a phrase of music assigned to different parts that begins one after the other.

Chromatic: notes that are a semitone apart or that are added to a scale to give colour.

Chord: three or more notes that are sounded together. A chord progression is a series of chords that may relate to each other because of the key they are played in.

Harmony: two or more notes that sound well together or the combination of chords that accompany a tune.

Key: the major or minor scales that give a name to a pattern of tones and semitones. Choosing a key for your music is important not only because of the pitch chosen but also because some keys have a particular colour to their sounds. The home note of the key is the first note of that scale and notes that do not belong to that key are said to be chromatic and they also add colour.

Syncopation: placing an accent on an unstressed note or using a rhythm made of groups of notes that clash with the underlying beat.

Theme: a short melody that is a musical idea that you can improvise with, write variations on or that you assign to a particular mood, moment or event.

Timbre: the tonal quality of the sound that identifies it.

Tone: this can be either the quality of the sound that is produced that can be attributed to an instrument, a voice or even a particular performer, or tone can be the distance of two semitones.

Unison: all playing or singing the same part, without any harmony.

Structure: the organisation of the musical ideas into a pattern of playing.

Word painting: using the pitch of the notes to enhance the meaning of the words.

Film score: music that is composed to specifically match the action, mood or emotion of a scene or an identifiable theme for the film as a whole.

Diegetic music: the music that is part of the action in the scene. For example, the band playing in the park, or the rehearsal music in a dance studio, or the music from a car radio.

Emotional impact music: the music that heightens the emotional state of the characters.

Pastiche: music written in the style of a specific era to set the scene of that time.

Comic music: music that closely follows the dramatic action such as a descending glissando for falling down, or using a muted trumpet for laughter, or pizzicato strings for creeping up on someone.

Underscore: the background music used under the dialogue.

Motif: a short piece of music to identify a particular location, character, scene or event.

Synchronisation: matching the sound with the shots.

c *Use Escher's art work to inspire your music*

Activities

5 Using only your voices, create the sounds of a human drum kit. Include base drum, snare and hi-hat. Aim to keep a steady beat by listening carefully to each other.

6 Now add a (vocal) bass guitar riff using three or four notes.

Activity

7 Look at the Escher painting (Photo **C**) and create an underscore to be played as a character explores the levels implied through illusion.

Use the following:

- chromatic patterns
- five-beat rhythm pattern
- varied timbre
- harmony
- chord.

Extension activity

You could challenge yourself to try counterpoint as two figures meet and part as they journey nowhere.

Research the film *Labyrinth* where you can see a multi-dimensional set that creates an Escher-inspired castle.

Conclusion

Having explored 'the family' through a diversity of stimuli and art forms, take time now to be clear about Contemporary Issues.

This is a compulsory Area of Study and although all of the sections of this chapter relate to various aspects of 'the family' there are many other issues that you may use for this area. Your teacher will guide you in your choice of an issue.

And finally ...

… just one more family story to complete your studies.

The Gilbert and Sullivan operetta *Ruddigore* is a story about the gallery of ancestors who come to life and step out of their portraits. They have to commit a daily crime or suffer an agonising death because of the curse on the Baronets of Ruddigore.

Although distinctly silly, it does highlight the pride of families who display their lineage in a portrait gallery. Recent interest in tracing family history has lead many people to discover their past, allowing real characters to stare out at the modern world from the posed photographic portraiture of the past. How could you work with your chosen art forms on the stimulus of ancestry?

A *The Gilbert and Sullivan operetta,* Ruddigore, *illustrated by Lucille Corcos, 1940*

3 From Past to Present

Starter activities

The lyrics of songs can clearly reference important events, whilst also quickly setting the social context of that generation. Read through the lyrics of 'Born in the Fifties' by the Police, from the album *Outlandos D'Amour* (1975). It is described as an anthem of the 'baby-boom generation'.

1. Who were the 'baby boomers' and when did the term become common language?
2. Name some of the important themes related to the baby boomers.
3. Who was John F. Kennedy?

> 66 *My mother cried/when President Kennedy died/She said it was the communists/but I knew better.* 99
>
> 66 *We were the class they couldn't teach/'cause we knew better.* 99
>
> 66 *Then we lost our faith and prayed to the TV/oh we should've known better.* 99

■ Political murder

In this chapter, you will find a range of art-form combinations, topics and arts works to study. Most relate to 'political murder' but the poem on page 68 is there to support the specimen examination paper (your teacher will have a copy of this). 'Motor racing', 'war', 'weddings' and 'historical events' are given at the end of the chapter on page 20 to broaden your understanding of topics that are From Past to Present study material.

Throughout history there have been those who sacrificed their lives because of their compelling need to express a personal viewpoint or refuse to adopt an imposed view. Such people had an amazing strength of will, tenacity and commitment. They provide us with strong characters to explore and, through the language of chosen art forms, experiment with the narratives of real people in real situations who met tragic ends. There have also been politicians and public figures who were murdered to show an individual or collective distaste for what they represented.

The following questions require a greater depth of understanding of the past, the political complexity and the power struggles of the world at that time.

4. Is the song questioning the political views of the older generation?
5. What significance do the Police see in the Kennedy assassination?
6. Is it simply an important event in the lives of baby boomers?

Just one verse of the song refers to the **assassination** of John F. Kennedy.

The phrase 'I knew better' is a recurring phrase in the lyrics and it is a good example of how repetition can give emphasis and security to engage the audience and focus on a specific aspect or attitude in the work. Look at the three separate lines from the song, shown left.

As you work through the examples in this chapter, you will:

- improve your ability to focus your research on those aspects of the stories of political murder in this chapter that have the potential to be developed into a performance or presentation.
- become aware of how the skills and techniques used in the art forms are able to communicate the event.

3.1 Dance and Drama

A story of dictatorship and death

On 2 December 2000, General Augusto Pinochet was tried in Chile on charges of kidnapping and murdering political opponents who 'disappeared' during his 17-year dictatorship.

For many years during General Pinochet's dictatorial reign in Chile, people who stood up to him were murdered or disappeared. Their fight for democracy was a very long one.

A *General Augusto Pinochet*

Christopher Bruce, a contemporary dance choreographer, created *Ghost Dances* in 1981 (see Photo **B**). It was a tribute to all of the people in Chile who fought for their freedom. He was inspired by their defiance. They believed in their cause and continued to rise against General Pinochet no matter how many times they were brought down. Bruce also wanted to show the suffering of the people.

There are many stories relating to General Pinochet's reign of power in Chile and how he manipulated his way into becoming a dictator. There are also many stories about his victims.

Objectives

Find out about the suffering of ordinary people under General Pinochet's dictatorship and use their stories as a starting point to create your own piece of dance/drama.

Study aspects of the dance work *Ghost Dances* and use this as a starting point to create a piece of dance/drama.

Activity

1 Choose one of the following options:

a Use *Ghost Dances* as a starting point to create a piece of dance and drama that tells your own story of people uprising against a political regime.

b Research various stories based on the life of General Pinochet or about the brave people who tried to oppose him and integrate dance into what you learn. Use *Ghost Dances* as a guide.

Short analysis of the opening dance in *Ghost Dances*

Christopher Bruce's *Ghost Dances* opens with a trio. Three men dressed as ghosts are representing the oppressors and/or Death. They are introducing us to the dance work and are creating the atmosphere. Their movements mainly consist of jumps, lifts and rolls on the floor. They use unison and some canon so the audience can identify with them.

After the initial sequence is danced in silence, the three ghosts perform movements that include folk steps to a haunting piece of music. Their focus is towards a light on the stage left side.

B   Ghost Dances, *Christopher Bruce, 1981*

The haunting music and the sharp angular movements of the dancers set against a backdrop of mountains create a very eerie feel and an air of suspense as to what might happen next.

The villagers enter from stage left and are unperturbed by the figures of death dancing. They might know what will happen next, or they might be prepared for their destinies.

Activity

2   Choose one of the following:

a   Watch the opening sequence of *Ghost Dances* and try to recreate some of the movements seen. Experiment with and manipulate the movements using different levels, speed and changes in direction. Using your manipulated or the original movement material, create several motifs that show how frightful 'Death' can be, e.g. the walking with flexed feet, patterns of actions followed by stillness or the off-stage focus.

b   The villagers dance to six different tunes, each one representing a different story where death will take one or more of them away. Pick one of the dances and **analyse** it in terms of movement content. Create your own dance that shows how villagers are being taken because of their beliefs.

If the dance you have created is already based on a **narrative**, you now need to extend this by creating a piece of drama that integrates with your dance.

AQA *Examiner's tip*

Do not sandwich your presentation. Make sure that the dance flows into a piece of drama and vice versa. A truly integrated presentation would tell the story with drama within the dance.

The beggar's dream

The poem below is by Mevlana Jalaluddin Rumi, a 13th-century Sufi poet. It was written in Persian and has been translated.

A Beggar Smiled at Me

A beggar smiled at me and offered me alms
In a dream last night, my heart sprang with delight
His beauty and grace which shone from his tattered
Presence took me by storm until I woke at dawn.
His poverty was riches, it covered my body in silk.
In that dream I heard the beckoning sighs of lovers,
I heard soft cries of agonizing joy saying: 'Take this,
Drink and be complete!' I saw before me a ring
Jewelled in poverty and then it nested on my ear.
From the root of my surging soul a hundred tremors
Rose as I was taken and pinned down by the surging sea.
Then heaven groaned with bliss and made a beggar of me.

Mevlana Jalaluddin Rumi, Divan 2015

Rumi shares some similarities with Shakespeare. Rumi produced a massive literary output which is still read today and the place that was most important in his life (in his case, Konya in Turkey) is still visited by thousands of admirers.

Rumi's life is fascinating. He was not only a poet, he was also a spiritual leader of the Mevlevi Brotherhood and he and his followers are closely associated with the ecstatic dance, or *sema*, of the Whirling Dervishes. The Dervishes perform to thousands of pilgrims in Konya on 17 December each year. This is known as Rumi's wedding night, or *urs*, when he passed into the presence of God.

Your Drama and Visual Arts piece, 'the beggar's dream' will use **images** from the poem as the starting point.

Drama

A good place to start your planning would be to create a narrative which could shape a Drama presentation.

Consider the following two phrases:

- A beggar smiled at me and offered me alms.
- His poverty was riches, it covered my body in silk.

These two images from the poem sum up the general meaning. The beggar who has nothing and is poor offers a kind of richness. The poem is also suggesting, therefore, that being rich is a kind of poverty. From investigation you would find that the ring he offers, that is worn in the ear, is the symbol of servitude.

A *A minaret at the shrine of Rumi*

Activity

1   Read the poem carefully.
a   Look up any words that you do not understand.
b   Highlight any images that might be useful for Drama.

Do not worry if you do not fully understand the meaning of the poem.

ur drama could use this rich/poor contrast as its theme.

e first four lines of the poem present the beggar as a visitor in dream, and as a result the dreamer feels amazingly uplifted – iritually richer, if you like.

ur drama could tell the story of someone who is visited in their eams by a spirit-beggar character, a bringer of happiness. The eamer could possibly be someone made miserable by their wealth d fame or power. Each dream-visit by the spirit beggar could provide :lue for the dreamer to take some action which would help to shed ⊇ burden of misery.

drama with two or three visits by a spirit beggar suggests a ucture of dream sequences, and dream sequences have great aginative and visual potential. Each dream could be based on image from the poem.

eam images from the poem include:

In that dream I heard the beckoning sighs of lovers.

I saw before me a ring/Jewelled in poverty.

I was taken and pinned down by the surging sea.

sual Arts

e spirit beggar is central to e dream drama and provides inspirational subject for an aginative costume design and e which could be constructed th low-cost materials. In pressive Arts, the designing and lisation of a costume is classed Visual Arts. You would need design and make the costume. e costume is all that is required.

B *An example of a design for a costume*

ctivity

Draw sketches of three alternative designs for the spirit-beggar character. Some suggestions are:

- A holy man/woman based on of the picture of a Sufi above.

- Combine dowdy rags to suggest a miserable poor beggar, and bright colours and patterns and a jaunty hat to suggest the bringer of happiness.

- A ghost-like spirit, male or female beggar, mostly white with grey smudges of dirt, a long grey or white wig, flowing robes or loose trousers.

xtension activity

vestigate Islamic border patterns. You could use them as a Visual Arts arting point. They were mostly used as the borders round texts.

ɔu could write a story (Original Writing) based on 'A Beggar Smiled at e' and present it in an illustrated and decorated book.

Activities

2 Look at the list of dream images from the poem and jot down ideas for dreams. Each scene should be a very different experience for the dreamer and develop the rich/poor theme. Link these ideas into a narrative sequence and try them out through drama improvisation.

3 Think of a good ending for the rich/poor theme. 'Then heaven . . . made a beggar of me' might suggest one.

Hint

Evidence in the Practical Portfolio or Working Processes

- Keep a log and take photographs of your drama improvisations.

- Provide sketches of your costume design ideas.

- Give reasons for choosing or rejecting each idea.

C *A Sufi offering gifts. Framed by a typical Islamic border pattern*

Moving Images and Drama

Throughout history murders have been committed for political motives. Sometimes the victims have been individual politicians, such as the Roman Emperor Julius Caesar or the American presidents Abraham Lincoln and John F. Kennedy. In other circumstances innocent victims have been murdered in their thousands or even millions, e.g. the Holocaust and the attempt by Khmer Rouge leader Pol Pot to form a Communist peasant farming society in Cambodia. Even today, in many parts of the world people are still being murdered for political reasons.

A Pieta, *Mark Balmer's painting of the murder of John F. Kennedy in Dallas in 1963. The President lies dying with his head in his wife's lap*

Activities

In your group, or working alone:

1 Create a list of politically motivated murders, in chronological order if possible, from earliest times until the present day.

2 Choose one event from the list, research the central character or characters, then using Drama and Moving Images create a short biopic of one major event in your character's life.

■ Practical exploration of the Holocaust

The Holocaust refers to the period starting in the 1930s when Adolf Hitler became chancellor of Germany until 1945 when the Second World War in Europe ended.

It was the systematic, state-sponsored persecution and murder of approximately six million Jews by the Nazi regime and its collaborators. 'Holocaust' is a word of Greek origin meaning 'sacrifice by fire'. The Nazi political doctrine stated that Germans were 'racially superior' and that the Jews, deemed 'inferior', were an alien threat to the so-called German racial community.

German authorities also targeted other groups because of their perceived 'racial inferiority': Roma (Gypsies), the disabled, and some of the Slavic peoples (Poles, Russians and others). Other groups were persecuted on political, ideological and behavioural grounds, among them Communists, Socialists, Jehovah's Witnesses and homosexuals.

This atrocity, the Final Solution, was planned on 20 January 1942 in a villa at Wannsee on the outskirts of Berlin. SS General Reinhard Heydrich, overall architect of the Final Solution, convened a meeting during which leading members of the SS and the Nazi government made definitive plans for the genocide of Europe's Jews. Ninety minutes later, the fate of millions of European Jews was sealed.

⬮⬮ links

Watch the clips from the film *Conspiracy* available at: www.youtube.com

Search for:
'conspiracy evacuation'
and
'conspiracy 60,000 Jews'

Activity

3   Watch the *Conspiracy* clips on YouTube and then discuss the following points with your group:

a   How are the people present at the meeting reacting to what is essentially a plan to murder millions on an industrial scale?

b   What use are they making of euphemisms, and why?

Your discussions will have given you a broader understanding of the topic of the Holocaust.

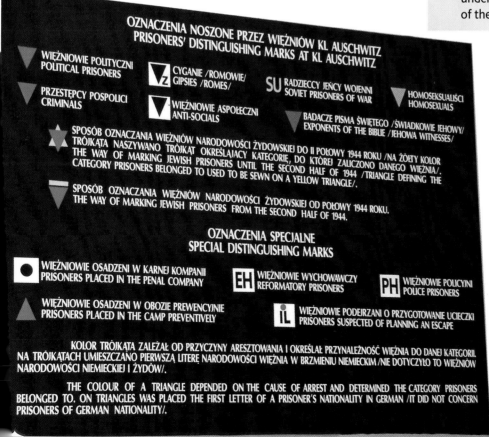

B   *Groups persecuted by the Nazis and sent to the Auschwitz-Birkenau concentration camps*

> 66 Do I think about those who died? Of course I do. I think of my mother and my sisters, of my niece and nephews, of all those children who never had a chance to live. I often wonder what the world has lost, what it will never have because those who died were on the verge of making their mark as doctors perhaps, or teachers, musicians, engineers. They all had so much to give and yet they were denied the chance. Even most of those who knew those people no longer exist. They have been wiped away as if they had never been known. I, who was lucky enough to survive, have a responsibility to ensure that they are never forgotten. 99
>
> *Arthur C. Benjamin,* Faces in the Smoke – The Story of Josef Perl, *Sylvia Perl, 2001 (the words of Josef Perl, a Holocaust survivor)*

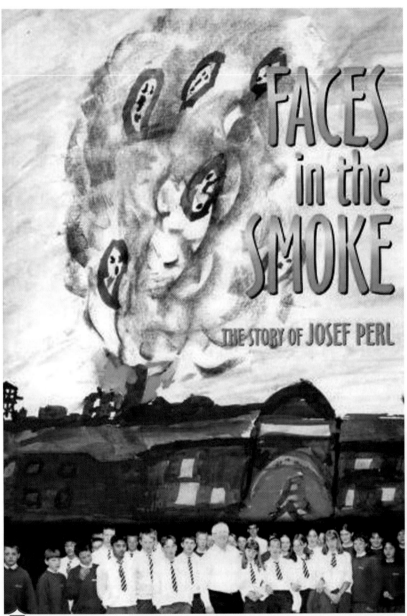

C Faces in the Smoke – The Story of Josef Perl

Hint

Take inspiration from the way in which professional directors create atmosphere in their films, e.g. Steven Spielberg's use of a **colour-pass** for the little girl's red coat in *Schindler's List*.

Photo **D** was taken in 2004 at the Auschwitz-Birkenau concentration camp in Poland. In this camp alone 1.5 million people were murdered, many of them children of your age or younger. In the background you can see one of the guard towers with the barbed-wire fencing in the foreground.

D   *Rose among thorns*

E   *These children were among the few remaining survivors when Auschwitz-Birkenau was liberated by the Russian army on 27 January 1945*

Activities

4   Using the material in this section and your own research, create a presentation combining Moving Images and Drama.

Here are some ideas to get you started:

■ Using the Photo **E** of the children liberated from Auschwitz-Birkenauh and the experiences of Josef Perl, create characters from your research and place them in a short docu-drama that you will film and edit.

■ Using the Photo **D** of the roses on the barbed wire, create an improvisation that reflects the mood of the image. Film and edit the piece in a way that enhances the atmosphere.

■ Choose a modern political murder or create your own scenario. Create the characters involved and film the incident in the style of a live news broadcast.

5

a   What is the significance of the roses in Photo **D**?

b   Why have they been placed with their heads hanging down?

c   Who might have placed them there?

∞ links

Books

Arthur C. Benjamin, *Faces in the Smoke – The Story of Josef Perl*, Sylvia Perl, 2001.

Eyewitness Auschwitz: Three Years in the Gas Chamber, Filip Muller, Ivan R. Dee Inc, 1999.

I have Lived a Thousand Years, Livia Bilton-Jackson, Simon & Schuster, 2000.

DVDs

Schindler's List (Universal Pictures).

Conspiracy (Warner Home Video).

Websites

www.ushmm.org (US Holocaust Memorial Museum).

www.bl.uk/learning/histcitizen/voices/holocaust.html

http://en.auschwitz.org.pl/m/ (Auschwitz-Birkenau Museum).

Jacques-Louis David (1748–1825) was a French painter who actively participated in radical politics and supported the French Revolution.

A The Death of Marat, *Jacques-Louis David, 1793*

The painting (**A**) depicts the political murder of Jean-Paul Marat, a French Revolutionist. Marat was murdered, whilst in his bath, by a supporter of the French monarchy Charlotte Corday (1768–93). The iconic romanticised view of him in this painting helped Marat to become a martyr after his death. Of course different audiences would react to this painting in different ways. A supporter of the French Revolution would have viewed the painting very differently to someone who did not support it.

Expressionist painter Edvard Munch (pronounced 'Moonk') created two paintings inspired by *The Death of Marat*. They were called *Death of Marat I and II*. Munch's paintings depict his own 'murder' at the hands of his lover, portraying deterioration in their relationship. Consider using a similar issue such as lost love or a relationship breakdown in your own investigation.

Objectives

Analyse and explore the study material: the painting *The Death of Marat* by Jacques-Louis David and the poem 'In Flanders Fields' by John McCrae.

Develop your ideas into a practical presentation using Visual Art and Original Writing.

∞ links

Visit www.edvard-munch.com

Activities

1. Produce a spider diagram to help develop your own theme in relation to political murder.

2. Sketch ideas for a piece of visual art inspired by *The Death of Marat*. You could sketch with pencils, charcoal, oil pastels, pen, or brush and ink.

AQA Examiner's tip

Early on in your planning think carefully about your intended audience and how this will influence your work.

∞ links

Refer to the section on acquiring skills in Chapter 1 (page 24) to remi[nd] yourself of everything you need to [do]

A famous poem from the First World War called 'In Flanders Fields' was inspired by the injustice of the dead soldiers and the hope that their fight would continue through the living.

In Flanders Fields

In Flanders fields the poppies blow
Between the crosses, row on row,
That mark our place; and in the sky
The larks, still bravely singing, fly
Scarce heard amid the guns below.

We are the Dead. Short days ago
We lived, felt dawn, saw sunset glow,
Loved and were loved, and now we lie
In Flanders fields.

Take up our quarrel with the foe:
To you from failing hands we throw
The torch; be yours to hold it high.
If ye break faith with us who die
We shall not sleep, though poppies grow
In Flanders fields.

John McCrae, May 1915

B *A Visual Arts interpretation of 'In Flanders Fields'*

John McCrae used various techniques in his poem to convey his political message and personal opinions on war:

- Notice the **rhyme scheme** of each **stanza** and how it is used to emphasise the **visual imagery** such as 'poppies blow … row on row'.
- McCrae places emphasis on 'We are the Dead' by ending the line mid-verse.
- The repetition of 'In Flanders fields' reminds the reader of the place where the dead soldiers lie.

This poem is rich in visual imagery, such as 'saw sunset glow', to help the reader empathise with the dead soldiers.

Extension activity

A poem called 'We Shall Keep the Faith' by Moina Michael was written in response to 'In Flanders Fields' three years later. The poem literally responds to 'In Flanders Fields' by representing the voice of the living, promising to honour the deaths of the soldiers. Read the poem at www.greatwar.co.uk/poems/faith.htm.

Consider using **call and response** in your work.

Activities

3 Write down key words from your Visual Arts ideas to create a piece of original writing which supports and responds to your art piece and reflects your ideas and point of view.

4 Using Visual Arts and Original Writing, create a presentation based on your own ideas from the theme 'political murder'. It is important to integrate your two art forms. For example, your Original Writing could be spoken aloud as the audience simultaneously watch a projection of your Visual Arts work. Or you could print political propaganda which would contain your Visual Arts and Original Writing.

AQA Examiner's tip

When creating your own Original Writing, visual imagery will help it integrate with your Visual Arts piece, particularly if the same imagery is reflected in both art forms.

Study newspaper articles and reports about 43-year-old Alexander Litvinenko and his subsequent death from multiple organ failure on 23 November 2006. You will also need to research and gain an understanding of polonium-210.

■ Polonium poisoning

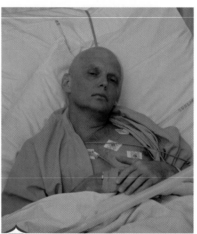

Alexander Litvinenko, a Russian who was living with his wife and young family in London, became ill and eventually died from polonium poisoning. It was a political murder and those investigating his death believe that he was deliberately given this radioactive substance in a cup of tea. The intention was that he would die, but not immediately, and that during the time he took to die, the evidence of poisoning would not be discovered.

A Alexander Litvinenko after he was poisoned

However, the murderers had not bargained on the tenacity of Alexander who, when he became ill, told the hospital that he may have been poisoned. He survived long enough for tests to be completed and for them to evidence his worst fears. It is thought that Alexander was targeted because he had formerly been an officer in the KGB (the Soviets Union's committee for state security) and he was living in London as a political exile.

Because it took some time to identify what was wrong with Alexander, the highly contaminating substance ^{210}Po that he had unknowingly ingested contaminated other people and places in London where Alexander and his murderers had been.

Opposite are some song lyrics to set to music. The aim of the lyrics is to advance the narrative in a dramatic work about Alexander Litvinenko. If you wish, you could write your own lyrics and set these to original music. The work from Activity 1 could also be used in this performance and this could be delivered by a narrator or used for a monologue. Your analysis of existing text will remind you of ways to give more than just facts. The emotive use of words will colour your work, and through careful phrasing, balance and pace you can build and shape the communication to support your creative intentions.

The important words in the first verse and chorus have been underlined and they should fall on the first beat of the bar. Taking four beats in a bar you will see that the first words do not fall on the first beat of the bar, making this phrasing **anacrusic**. The verse is eight bars long.

The chorus is four bars long and a quaver rhythm will give it more pace. 'Mean to me' could be one-beat notes for emphasis. Look at Diagram **C** for an illustration of the rhythm.

B Radiation symbol

Polonium

It is |here already, in |very small amounts
in our |bodies, the soil and the |air.
But to |hide a large dose in a |simple cup of tea,
Can|not be considered to be |fair

But do I |care, I wasn't there,
what does this |mean to me?
I was |out eating Sushi
not |drinking cups of Tea.

Discovered by Marie Curie in 1898,
this isotope is lethal yet evasive.
It cannot be seen, tasted or smelt
yet in our bodies, it is very invasive.

But do I care, I wasn't there,
what does this mean to me?
I was out eating Sushi
not drinking cups of Tea

I was reading of Alexander who was slowly dying.
Deterioration, contamination and losing all his hair.
I'd been out with my friends at a Sushi Bar
Now I read they've found polonium there!

Yes, now I care, I was there,
this means something to me.
I was out eating Sushi
not drinking cups of Tea.

Activity

2   Decide on the mood you require for the song 'Polonium'. It is not a very nice story and it suggests menacing pulsing music.

Explore accompaniment styles. Ask your teacher to play you some, e.g. Stephen Sondheim's song 'The Ballad of Sweeney Todd'. The opening intro is like a murmur of death and this may give you some ideas.

Say the lyrics to yourself to establish the natural rhythm of the words and to find the important words. These will naturally fall on the first beat of the bar. This has been done for you in verse 1 and the chorus. Now complete the accents for the whole song.

Your voice will have a natural tendency to rise and fall with the meaning of the words and this will help you to compose a melody and to make use of **word painting**.

The chorus is somewhat flippant, and was written as a relief from the serious content of the verses. This provides an opportunity to lighten the mood perhaps by changing both the harmony and the accompaniment pattern.

Finally there is a 'sting' to this tale. How will you handle the ending. Remember you are aiming to be not only creative and expressive but innovative (see Chapter 4).

Extension activity

Find a copy of the poem 'A Poison Tree' by William Blake. It communicates the hatred and anger that can lead to a lack of remorse at the death of another. Anger can grow and when hidden it can become a deadly poison.

The opening verse is simple and memorable yet it does communicate very effectively the hidden meaning disguised in its simplicity.

The opening song 'The Ballad of Sweeney Todd' from the musical *Sweeney Todd* by Sondheim is also a good arts work for study. The character Sweeney is intent on revenge for the injustice he suffered at the hands of the judge, but seeking his revenge led him to kill many more people.

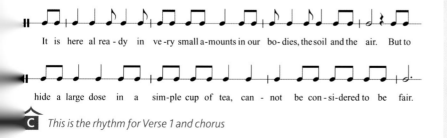

It is here al rea - dy   in   ve -ry small a-mounts in our bo- dies, the soil and the air.   But to
hide a large dose   in   a   sim-ple cup of tea, can - not   be con-si-dered to be   fair.

C   *This is the rhythm for Verse 1 and chorus*

3.6 Music and Dance

Murder at the cathedral

On 29 December 1170, the Archbishop of Canterbury, Thomas Becket, was murdered in the cathedral. This political murder remains one of the most well-known episodes in English history.

King Henry II and Thomas Becket had been old friends and the King made Becket Archbishop in 1162. The King had differences with the Pope and he wanted Becket, as Archbishop, to support him.

But Becket argued and disagreed with the King, making him so angry that Becket fled to France. They later made up their differences, but when Becket criticised the King, Henry shouted to his knights: 'Will no one rid me of this troublesome priest?' Four knights rode to Canterbury and killed Becket in the cathedral. The candle in Photo **A** marks the original place of Thomas Becket's shrine.

It is a good story and because of this it has the potential to be explored and developed into a presentation with strong characters, mood, emotion and atmosphere.

A *Trinity Chapel, Canterbury Cathedral*

Linking to the activities above, the Archbishop could travel in a very calm, purposeful and direct manner. The music to accompany this could be a solemn progression of chords.

A knight could be strong, bold and flamboyant with dynamic, bright music reflecting the glinting light on the sword.

B *Music to accompany the Archbishop*

Objectives

Generate ideas from the study material: the poem *Murmurings and Martyrdom*.

Develop them into a practical presentation combining Music and Dance.

Activities

In your group or working alone:

1. Consider a sequence of events arising from this political murder.

2. Identify the character(s) you could create through music and dance.

3. Link a character to a short music idea and devise a travelling dance motif to match this.

AQA Examiner's tip

Be adventurous; develop your own, unique language of combined arts. Think of the performance as 'weaving' Music and Dance together, with both art forms working in total unity to communicate your aim to the audience.

Murmurings and Martyrdom

Where Falcons rest
a watching, waiting silence falls.
Echoes break the stillness of the night.

Glints of steel, chinks of armour.

With senses tight as gut
the Canterbury women watch;
with waiting dread they listen.

Scurries and scuffles of scavenging vermin:
Are there morsels of flesh, is there thirst slaking blood
to be spilt on the sacred flagstones?
'Will no one rid me of this troublesome priest?'

In dim light pierced by a sudden, silent scream
the huddled women freeze.
Percussive armour rattles and resounds
from unforgiving walls.
A silhouetted body slumps
entombed within the shadows of the vault.

The stink of death
is creeping like a mist.
The deed is done.
Tarnished swords evaporate.

Motionless, forlorn,
the women's wails and lamentations
soar to a crescendo in the keening roof
and twist and spiral round the columns;
thunderous tendrils barbed with thorns.

From brittle life,
broken,
shattered by four brutal blows,
enduring martyrdom is born.

Activity

4   Read through the poem 'Murmurings and Martyrdom'. Choose two sections of the text and explore them through the language of music and dance. Here are two ideas to get you started:

■   A short phrase of music, using 'Echoes break the stillness of the night' for inspiration. Take the chord of A minor and over a sustained A or an **ostinato** on A, use other notes of the chord to represent the echoes breaking the stillness. You could use the rhythm of the word 'e-choes' for your chosen notes and change the pitch or fade the dynamic to colour your idea.

■   A dance motif taking inspiration from 'and twist and spiral round the columns'. Use spiralling arm movements around a twisting torso. Once secured, explore travelling in the motif or turning out of the motif.

You are aiming to come up with an idea that is distinctly your own, different and ideally suited to your chosen interpretation of the study material. You should identify the skills that you need to work on so that you can realise your creative ideas.

C   *Music to accompany a knight*

Conclusion

You will have seen how this area of study gives you the opportunity to relate to a specific historical event and through your knowledge and understanding of your chosen art forms share your performance or presentation with a target audience of your choice.

To complete your exploration of this topic, political murder, below is a really tasty yet dangerous story.

Lucrezia Borgia

The Borgias were a family of Spanish descent who moved to Italy during the late Renaissance. In the 1400s Italy had many city-states and rival fiefdoms that were constantly waging war and committing murder for land, wealth and power.

Lucrezia Borgia was a beautiful yet **manipulative** member of this infamous family and she is said to have had a hollow ring that she used to poison drinks. Dining with the Borgias may have been a very dangerous social activity as Lucrezia was said to employ both a chef and a poisoner to take care of her guests.

This is a great story with the potential for strong characters from which to create drama, dance and music. Imagine the 'dance of death' of the social climbers in this dangerous society who never made it home from the party!

A Portrait of a Woman *by Bartolomeo Veneziano, c.1500, traditionally assumed to be Lucrezia Borgia*

4 Peoples and places

Objectives

Take inspiration from a place or the culture of that place.

Understand the arts of that culture and use this to inform your presentation.

■ Identifying different peoples and places

The arts works of specific **cultures** are often very clearly identifiable due to their distinctive style. You may be surprised by how much you already know about the world's diverse cultures.

Starter activity

1   For each of the following peoples and places topics give two signifiers and assign each to an art form:

a   African tribes

b   Aboriginal people

c   Persian carpets.

For example, Carnival in Rio – colourful costumes (Visual Arts) and dancing in the streets (Music and Dance).

Identify the peoples and places in the images shown in Photo **A**.

A *Peoples and places*

The photographs of amazing places in the world can provide excellent starting points for Expressive Arts, e.g. *Cueva del Fantasma* ('The Cave of the Ghost'). This is an enormous cave (so big that helicopters can fly into it) in southern Venezuela in one of the most inaccessible and unexplored regions of the world.

⚭ links

Search on the internet for 'Explorers discover huge cave in Venezuela'. On the msnbc link you can see a photo of the Cueva del Fantasma.

Video dance

The Expressive Arts performance to be developed in this section requires a group of no more than five. Each student should choose a combination of Dance, Moving Images and mask making (Visual Arts). It is possible for most members of the group to choose Dance and Moving Images as their two art forms. Only one mask is necessary but more could be made. One or more members of the group could choose mask making as their second art form or it could be an additional art form.

The masks are to be made first and they will then feature in a dance which is filmed. Not every mask made has to be used in the dance. The camera operator must be prepared to move with the dancers so that the camera's view becomes a part of the dance. In this way the three elements become fully integrated into a screened presentation.

There is a fourth element: music. The music could be original and created by the group, but there are some suitable native North American-style recordings available and these could be found and selected. Two suggestions are: *Raindance* (produced by PolyGram TV) and *Sacred Spirit* (produced by Virgin Records).

North American masks and their stories

Each native North American tribe uses masks that differ in design and purpose according to their traditions – traditions which are continued by modern-day craftsmen. Some of the most beautiful are those carved in wood with coloured surface decorations. The most spectacular are transformation masks which open up to reveal masks within masks. These can be more than two metres high, but they can also be simple corn husk masks (see Cartoon **A**). The masks were worn in ceremonies and dances, such as at initiations into adulthood, usually by a shaman at a winter potlatch, and they linked the community with the spirit world. They represented sky, sea and water spirits, ancestors and dead warriors, mythical creatures and characters, animal and bird spirits.

A *Corn husk mask, Iroquois people, north-eastern United States*

Cartoon **B** (the cannibal woman) is a good example. The *Dzunukwa*, or cannibal woman, is a dangerous monster. Twice the height of a normal person, with a black, hairy body and sagging breasts, she lurks in the forest and eats children. The dancer wearing the mask moves clumsily to represent the monster's confusion outside the forest environment.

After carrying out your own study of North American masks and their stories, design and make the mask/s that can be worn or carried in a ceremonial dance. Techniques for constructing masks can easily be found.

Activity

Find out about:

- North American masks.
- Masks and dance.
- Shamanism.
- Initiation ceremonies into adulthood.
- Potlatch.
- Mask making.

The dance, the camera, the editing

Guidance about how to choreograph a group dance by developing ideas from dance motifs is given on pages 78–9.

For this video dance, the following ideas should be explored both in the creation of the initial motifs and in the development of the structure:

B *Cannibal woman mask, Kwakiutl people, Vancouver Island, British Columbia*

- The stories that are associated with the masks can give the dance a narrative structure and the ways that the characters in the stories move can be a starting point for motifs.

- Practise wearing or handling a mask when moving: the way that the mask sits on your head, the limitations of looking through eyeholes or moving a large mask from one hand to the other will dictate how you move. Inevitably the movements will have to be kept simple and stylised.

- Experiment with the camera being part of the dance so that the camera then becomes a dancer's eye view. The operator needs to develop confidence in moving and holding the camera. The camera can change levels in the same way that a dancer does. The camera can look through the eyeholes of a mask. Other dancers can approach or circle the camera and the camera can approach or circle other dancers.

- Experiment with using extreme close-ups of very small movements so that gestures of just hands or arms or feet, or tilts of the head/mask, fill the screen and become a part of the overall choreographic plan.

- After experimenting with and improving your skill in the above techniques develop your ideas into a choreographic plan and create a storyboard.

- The choreographic plan could include some special video effects and layered images.

- Synchronising the sequence of shots and effects with the music will demand some skilful editing, so you will need to experiment in order to get this right.

Because the dance is divided up into shots and does not have to be performed as one sequence, with careful planning it is possible for members of the group to work in their two art forms – to perform as dancers and in the roles required for video production (camera work and editing). One student could be the choreographer/director.

The finished piece will be a video presentation and there is scope for some very creative and adventurous camera, editing and dance work. The masks will make it visually stunning.

Hint

Evidence in the Practical Portfolio

Keep a log of your work as it develops, and take photographs (or capture still images) of:

- the design and construction of a mask
- the creation of dance motifs
- experiments with a hand held camera as part of the dance
- experiments with extreme close ups
- experiments with video effects.

Include any first drafts and the final storyboard of the choreographic plan.

Attach a DVD showing short extracts of experimental work (this must be no longer than five minutes' duration).

Write evaluative comments about:

- reasons for choosing or rejecting any of the results of experiments
- how effectively the final edited video presentation communicates with an audience.

4.2 — Drama and Dance

The spirits of the stones

The places that people use to pay homage to the sun, moon and stars, and the monuments erected down the ages, become potent with mystery and power.

A Stonehenge *by John Constable, 1835*

In this painting of Stonehenge the mysteriousness of the huge forms and the spaces around them are accentuated by the dramatic light and weather conditions depicted. It would make an exciting and atmospheric film or stage setting.

This Drama and Dance piece, 'the spirits of the stones', will use the following images from the painting as starting points:

- the shapes and forms of the standing and fallen stones
- the darkening, threatening stormy conditions depicted and the shafts of light/energy
- the two isolated characters dwarfed by the stones.

Dance

A good starting point would be to create a dance which expresses the atmosphere of the great stones. It will be a solemn, ceremonial, processional dance with slow-moving motifs. It could be accompanied by sustained chords, humming or contemplative music. (Some suggestions for music are: Gregorian chant; Erik Satie, 'Gymnopédie' or 'Gnossienne'; Olivier Messiaen, 'Gagaku', Part Five of 'Oiseaux Exotiques' – a piece inspired by exotic birds and exotic places around the world; Alex North, in *2001 A Space Odyssey* and particularly the music by Gyorgy Ligeti that signifies the advancement of learning.)

Objectives

Generate ideas and develop them into a practical presentation which combines Drama and Dance in response to ancient standing stones.

Analyse and explore the study material: the painting *Stonehenge* by John Constable.

Activity

1   Jot down notes about how you might create a set for a performance combining Drama and Dance that suggests the atmosphere and structures of the painting. You could use quite simple materials such as projected images, stage blocks and drapes, and lighting to create the striking effects of light and shade.

Activity

2   Consider the two people in *Stonehenge* and create a narrative about either:

- 'new-age' type characters who are seeking unity with cosmic energies. One has psychic tendencies and is seriously freaked out by the 'spirits', or

- ramblers who find a dead body among the stones. There could be some interesting interaction between the 'spirits' and the dead person.

In both cases the characters will be spooked by unaccountably scary happenings and sensations, and actors will have to communicate that the 'spirits' are invisible.

Drama

The drama should be a sharp contrast to the dance so that the dance and the drama work in **counterpoint**. The drama could even be funny and would be best set as darkness approaches.

For Expressive Arts practical work you are allowed to work in a group of no more than five. If everyone is contributing Dance and Drama you will have to make smooth transitions between being actor or dancer. With places to hide on stage – behind the stones – this should be possible without leaving the stage.

It would work even better if some members contribute set design (Visual Arts), Music or script writing (Original Writing) as one of their art forms.

B *'New Age' psychic character is spooked by dancing spirits*

Activity

3 In your dance space build a temporary set which suggests the stones using stage blocks or an arrangement of chairs; they can represent standing or fallen stones – be careful!

■ Play your chosen music.

■ Each person in the group should choose a spot facing a 'stone'. Imagine what it would really look like, and take your position at high, medium or floor level in response to the mass and power of the stone – you could think of it having a character.

■ As the music plays, slowly change to a second and then a third position – each position should change level and change its relationship to the front so that the 'stone' is at your side or behind you.

■ Add slow, processional steps between the positions.

■ Repeat this until it becomes a fluent sequence with slight pauses at the positions.

■ The steps might take you on a journey around the dance space, but try and come back to the start point so that the dance can become cyclical.

■ Two dancers at a time, perform your sequence with others in the group watching.

■ When you have completed the Dance Improvisation Activity you will have enough material to choreograph a group dance among the stones. Learn each other's sequences and perform them in unison or in cannon and with interaction between the dancers.

■ This dance could represent spirits of the past who are a continuous part of this place – they are its mysterious atmosphere.

■ If the Dance represents spirits of the past then the Drama could be in the present. Throughout the rest of the piece there could be some interaction between the 'invisible' spirit dancers and the action of the drama set in this place.

Hint

Evidence in the Practical Portfolio or Working Processes

Keep a log and take photographs as you develop the characters and the narrative of the drama.

Using diagrams, record the floor patterns of the dance, photograph the 'positions', make video clips of developing motifs.

Write evaluative comments about:

■ dance positions and their relationship with the forms of stones

■ developing a contrapuntal composition mixing comic drama and solemn dance.

Extension activity

Investigate the paneurythmic dancing of the White Brotherhood in the Rila Mountains, Bulgaria. The White Brotherhood come together once each year to greet and honour the rising sun and celebrate its spiritual significance with a mass ritual of dance and chanting.

You could use this as a starting point for choreographing a processional dance.

Posters

Although we tend to think of **advertising** as the promotion of products, it can take many other forms including propaganda. This is the spreading of information aimed at influencing the opinions or behaviour of large numbers of people. Instead of impartially providing information, propaganda aims to influence its audience by being selective in its presentation of the facts. The object is to produce an emotional rather than rational response to the information presented in order to further a, usually, political agenda.

Study the two posters in Photo **A** and discuss the following points with your group:

- The use of colour – what does it symbolise in each case?
- The use of the main image in each case – how do the posters differ in their approach?
- How does each poster put a different emphasis on winning the war against the Nazis and how does this reflect the culture of the society that produced it?

A *Two propaganda posters from the Second World War*

Magazine advertisements

Study Wella's magazine advertisement (Photo **B**) and note these points:

1. The placing of the three characters to draw the eye of the viewer to the boy's hair.
2. The use of the humorous **double entendre**: 'The girls were falling for Andy. But Andy's hair wasn't falling for anyone.'
3. The use of the game-style 'Shockwaves. STYLE. ATTRACT. PL>Y'.
4. The prominent positioning of the product.

B *A Shockwaves advert by Wella*

Activities

2 What is the specific target group for this advertisement?

3 Discuss your decision with your group and give your reasons for your choice.

4 Collect a range of magazine advertisements that you consider to be effective. Share your findings and discuss your reasons with your group.

■ Television and film advertising

The average length of a television commercial is between 30 and 60 seconds. In this short time the advertiser has to show the product, create the need in the customer for the product, and possibly give details of price and availability. Not an easy task! The advertiser uses various techniques to help get the message across, from a careful choice of style, to **piggybacking**, **reinforcement** and **pack-shots**.

C *A still from the Pride Oil advertisement*

Activity

5 You should now have a good working knowledge of what elements make an effective advertisement, so in your group or working alone choose to develop one of the following:

a Create your own original product to advertise. Use your visual arts skills to design and make the packaging for the product and possibly a point-of-sale display or magazine advertisement. Use these objects in your advertisement which you will film and edit. Remember, you should aim to make your advert 45 seconds long.

b Choose a film **genre** and use your Visual Arts skills to create a movie poster and DVD cover for the original film trailer that you will film and edit. You have a target length of two minutes for your trailer.

Extension activity

Plan, film and edit a short promotional video about your school to raise awareness within the local community. Produce posters for display in local shops and businesses, stating when and where the programme can be seen, or from whom copies can be obtained. If you can negotiate a budget with your head teacher, you might like to create a display advertisement for your local newspaper in order to reach a wider audience.

∞ links

Visit www.youtube.com watch the Pride Oil advertisement. Search for: pride oil wmv.wmv. It is a good example of piggy-backing as it is based on the very popular Bollywood film *Kabhi Khushi, Kabhie Gham* and is almost identical in places. It also demonstrates the effective use of pack-shots and reinforcement. As you watch the advertisement, count how many times you see, or hear, the words 'Pride' or 'Pride Oil'.

You can watch a short clip from *Kabhi Khushi, Kabhie Gham* by searching the title on YouTube.

∞ links

Another example of piggy-backing can be found on YouTube. Search for: pepsi we will rock you, to see an advert based on the Ridley Scott film *Gladiator*.

AQA *Examiner's tip*

Be imaginative in your choice of product or film genre.

Make sure that you include the appropriate techniques learnt in this chapter, such as identifying a clearly defined **target group**.

In a 45-second advertisement all of your shots and editing need to be very accurate.

Excite and tempt your audience, but do not give away too much of the plot in your film trailer, otherwise no one will purchase the DVD!

4

Conclusion

Exploring the **traditions** and cultures of Peoples and Places will broaden your knowledge and understanding of the world. We live in a global society and in this modern world there can be no excuse for misunderstanding the culture and traditions of different peoples. The recording of their heritage is heavily entrenched in the arts.

Music

The distinctive use of melody, harmony and instruments in world music is now recognised by the Recording Academy as a World Music Grammy Award category that includes international, non-Western classical music and international non-American and non-British traditional folk music.

Visual Arts

Visual Arts are paintings, sculpture, traditional costumes, architecture and decorative arts that take inspiration for their cultural traditions.

Dance

Folk dance and social dance from different regions of the world inspire dancers to combine movement elements and symbolism with contemporary dance.

Drama

Dramatic storytelling has roots in many cultures. The Japanese dance-drama *Kabuki* is a highly stylised way of telling a story and the visual art of *Kumadori* make-up is an essential component. *Kumadori* puppetry also makes a link to visual arts.

AQA Examiner's tip

Do absorb the cultural traditions you are studying and include them in your work.

⚭ links

See www.glopac.org and search the GloPAD (Database) for examples of *Kumadori* make-up.

Revision activity

Working with your two chosen art forms research one of the peoples or places in the Starter activity on page 81 and explore the performance/presentation possibilities arising from your understanding of that culture.

It is important to realise that you do not need to copy the specific style of the peoples or places topic you have studied. You will need to understand this style in its geographical context and use this knowledge to create work perhaps from the same starting point or belief of the study material.

A Kumadori *faces*

5 Universal Themes

▪ Taking charge in a Universal Theme arts work

Creating a presentation from a theme has always been a very popular part of the Expressive Arts examination. This is probably because it allows you greater freedom to respond to the theme and develop it as you wish. The creative route that you choose to follow will be specific to your art forms and ideas, your experiences and the links that you make to feelings, emotions and the 'whimsical'.

Many questions will be spinning around in your head and you will need to put them in order and refine your thoughts to answer them.

Now is a good time to look back at Chapter 1. You have come a long way since working with the theme 'a journey'. Your experiences will have given you a method of working that will ensure that you can generate your own ideas to work with and be confident in the outcome. Remember the IDEAS mnemonic:

Investigate the study sources chosen and your exploration will lead you to:

Develop ideas that will enable you to use the material.

Explain your train of thought in your portfolio of evidence and

Analyse by breaking it down into its component images.

Select those that are best suited to achieving your aim.

Be confident and find your own way forward. Take ownership of the task and develop ideas for your presentation.

The following examples of Universal Themes that appear in this chapter and the art forms assigned to them:

'The window': Visual Arts and Dance, page 90–1.

'Winter': Original Writing and Moving Images, page 92–3.

'The sea': Music and Moving Images, page 94–5.

'A journey': all art-form combinations are possible.

This was studied in Chapter 1, page 20–1.

The composition draws your eye to the people through the window and their vulnerability.

Nighthawks (Photo **A**) was inspired by a diner in Manhattan and was painted just after the Japanese attacked Pearl Harbor and brought the Americans into the Second World War.

Notice how the 'nighthawks' sit trapped inside the diner with no exit. Their hunched shoulders portray their tension and the bright lights make them look as if they are on display to the rest of the city. The barman is also trapped inside his bar. A lonely New York street takes up over half of the painting.

Edward Hopper (1882–1967) was an American artist who studied illustration in New York. He painted in the style known as **realism**. He painted streets, buildings, petrol stations and the people who inhabited them. Most of his paintings focus on the relationship we have with our environment and with one another.

Objectives

Explore Universal Theme 'The Window' through the study material: *Nighthawks*, a painting by Edward Hopper, and the contemporary dance-drama *Swansong*, choreographed by Christopher Bruce.

Develop your ideas into a practical presentation combining Visual Arts and Dance.

A Nighthawks, *Edward Hopper, 1942*

Activity

1. Edward Hopper's paintings have inspired many film scenes and set designs.

   Sketch some ideas for a cityscape or set design where a window or windows are the main element. You could use apartment windows, a shop window or as in the painting, a diner window. Restrict your design to looking into the building through a window. If you are working on a set design, you could think about how to use lighting and gauzes for effect. Then explore and develop your ideas by looking out of the window onto the city street.

Hint

Looking *in* through a window will give very diferent ideas to looking *out* of the window.

∞ links

Nighthawks was parodied in *The Simpsons*. To learn more visit http://en.wikipedia.org and search: homer vs. the eighteenth amendment.

Swansong

wansong by Christopher Bruce was created for
e English National Ballet in 1987. It is based in
art on the writing of Oriana Fallaci and explores
e interrogation and torture of a prisoner by
vo guards. The subject is as relevant today as
hen it was created and it shows how dance can
ommunicate political awareness as well as being
eautiful and engaging choreography. There is
rigour in its composition and simplicity in the
ay the three dancers relate that successfully
ommunicates a depth of meaning. Combining
ontemporary dance, classical line, a soft shoe
nuffle and a brief suggestion of a tango gives strong
motional impact and this is complemented by
usic composed for the work.

begins with the prisoner slumped on a chair on a
are stage with a window high up at the side, letting
a stream of light. The two suave interrogators are
ressed in khaki shirts and trousers. The attacking
ound of a slamming prison door followed by the
ng echoing decay of that sound, initiates the
owing continuity of movement and lifts performed
y the three dancers. Through a series of episodes,
e two interrogators tease and torment the prisoner
sing Vaudeville-like routines tainted with brutality.
those moments when they leave the stage, the
risoner imagines the freedom that lies beyond the
indow. Christopher Bruce leaves the audience free
interpret the work and it could be that at the end
s soul is released from his body to escape through
e window to freedom.

Activity

3 Watch an extract from *Swansong* (either on
YouTube or on DVD) where all three dancers are
performing and pay particular attention to the
way they relate to each other.

■ Working in a trio, create a short phrase of
movement where the group members are
constantly moving around, under and over each
other. Conclude this with a moment of stillness,
and then repeat the phrase of movement.

■ Expand this trio work by modifying your
choreography to communicate to the audience
that two group members are dominant.

■ Develop your choreography by expanding the
skills you are using. Consider the giving and
taking of weight, turning, floor work, circling and
spiralling movements initiated through touch
and the skill of stopping with control, in unison
to hold an image of stillness.

Activity

2 Combining visual arts and dance, create a
presentation or performance inspired by
the theme of 'the window'. Use ideas from
your study of *Nighthawks* and *Swansong* and
remember that visual arts to integrate with
dance could be costume design, props, a
backdrop, set design or a sculpture that becomes
an integral part of the presentation.

You may wish to consider:

■ Stepping through a window of time to put
something right.

■ A window that becomes a time portal to access
the future.

■ Shop window mannequins who tire of looking
out of their window and who find a way joining
the real world.

■ A window of opportunity that opens briefly.

■ The view from a famous window.

B *The light from the prison cell window adds meaning to
the scene*

AQA Examiner's tip

Take time to refine your combined arts work. Organise
the content so that you communicate effectively to
the chosen audience.

'Manisha and the Mystery Christmas Card'

The theme of 'winter' has inspired many arts works. Among them are paintings like Photo **A** *Homecoming by the Winter Woods*, which appear as the subject of seasonal cards sent to celebrate the Christian festival of Christmas. This task is based on this idea and tells the story of 'Manisha and the Mystery Christmas Card' using Original Writing to write a script for a short film (Moving Images).

The beginning of the story

Manisha was a lonely girl, and she had no one she could really call a friend. Being a Hindu it was doubly unexpected that she should receive a Christmas card. The card was a beautiful winter scene, showing three people dressed in old-fashioned clothes walking through a wood with deep snow on the ground. Inside, after the printed greetings, it was signed 'M' something. It was a short name, but the letters after the 'M' were badly smudged – she hoped not by a tear. Manisha could not think of anyone she knew with a name beginning with 'M' – except her own. As she looked closely at the picture on the card she tried hard to recall meeting a stranger who might have had a name beginning with 'M'. The first accidental meeting she remembered was in the park. Her mother, as she so often did, had left her alone on a park bench and nearby a girl, with her father, was trying to launch a kite. After several failed attempts the kite took off and started to dance in the sky. Then, on a gust and a swirl of wind, the kite quite suddenly and unexpectedly crashed onto the seat next to her, missing her by millimetres. The girl, giggling but very apologetic, came running over to her.

This is the first of three encounters with strangers that Manisha recalls and she was not sure that any of them had names beginning with 'M'.

A *Homecoming by the Winter Woods, Adolph Kaufmann*

Objectives

Generate ideas and develop them into a practical presentation which combines Original Writing and Moving Images in response to the theme of 'Winter'.

Activity

Moving Images

1. In your group, make up the next two 'encounters' that Manisha had and write down the story in the form of a storyboard. Keep in mind simple locations where you can easily use a video camera, and think about the number of actors that you have available for additional characters.

   a Check out the locations.

   b Check out availability of cameras.

   c Work out a shooting schedule and allocate production jobs to members of the group.

   You are now in a position to begin writing the script.

Activity

Original writing

2 Prepare a script storyboard on a sheet of A4 (landscape) using Table **B** as a template. If you keep to just three camera shots on each sheet there is plenty of room for you to write the script and link each section of script to a specific shot. You do not have to use the sample script, but it might help to get you started. Be prepared to rewrite the script several times. Try it out each time with your group in a rehearsal and be ready to make a note of their suggestions for improvements. In the end, however, it is your script and your group must listen to your ideas. You will negotiate creative solutions to problems together – this is an essential part of group work in Expressive Arts.

Hint

Evidence in the Practical Portfolio

Keep script storyboards with early versions of the script to show how it was amended and improved as your group tried it out and changes were made. Write notes which give reasons for the amendments that you make.

B   *Sample script storyboard*

Location/Action	Camera/Sound	Dialogue
	'Winter music' **1 CU** of inside the card.	MANISHA: (*voice over*) What could the name be? Meg, Mel, Maggie, Maddie? I d'know. S'pose it could be a boy. No, no *boy* would send a card to me. In fact, I don't know *anyone* who would send a card to me. But someone has. It's a bit embarrassing really, not knowing who it's from. It's sad. Who could it be? If I can work it out I'll send them a card back and then we could arrange to meet up sometime – if Mum would let me.
	2 CU of picture. **3** Zoom in till image goes out of focus. *'Winter music cross-fades to going-into-your-head music'.*	MANISHA: (*voice over*) Perhaps Mum would let me invite her here. It's a lovely picture. Lovely snow and trees – just like it should be.
	'Going into your head music as . . .' Zoom out from fuzzy focus to . . . **4 LS** Manisha on park bench.	MANISHA: (*voice over*) I remember seeing someone a few days ago when I was left on my own on a bench, one on the big field in the park. Mum had gone off shopping and just left me as she often did. I get on her nerves when she is seriously shopping. There was a girl with her dad trying out a kite in the wind. I wish my dad was around. It's a really colourful kite. I wonder where she got it. Oh help I think it's going to land on me!

Notes on the music

The 'Camera/Sound' instructions for the first storyboard frame in Table **B** mention 'Winter music'. Listen to the Largo movement of 'Winter' from *The Four Seasons* by Antonio Vivaldi. You could use this as very quiet background music mixed with the voiceover.

The 'Camera/Sound' instructions also refer to 'going-into-your-head' music. The convention is to use swirling harp arpeggios, but these might be difficult to find.

These are just ideas. Someone in the group might like to compose and play original music instead.

Extension activity

Look at Photo **A**, *Homecoming by the Winter Woods*. You will see three figures – a man, a woman and a child. Using these as your main characters and the title: 'Homecoming by the Winter Woods', write the outline of a story that could be adapted for a short film and write the script using the techniques outlined here.

Study material

Work with the main theme music for the film *Jaws*. This is an example of how John Williams' memorable score sets the tone of impending terror. The music is just as responsible for the power of the film as the moving images of the shark itself.

John Williams' score for Steven Spielberg's big success *Jaws* has been described as 'the ideal marriage between film director and composer'. The music is a chilling and scary complement to the disturbing visual images and it gave the film a creative voice that the limited special effects could not achieve alone. When you watch and analyse the scenes where you actually see the shark you will realise that without the music the impact of the moving images would be considerably diminished. The simple main theme is played on cello and bass with its pulsing driving rhythm played during the opening credits followed by underwater shots of the shark. In the opening scene the images of a young girl skinny-dipping at night and her unexpected murder by the shark is the most remembered scene from this film.

The poster in Photo **A** shows the shark's gigantic, pointed head positioned vertically and a dark mouth filled with jagged teeth.

The mechanical shark that they used in the film was affectionately called 'Bruce' after Spielberg's lawyer. They had problems with Bruce (the shark!) who had a tendency to sink, and Spielberg asked John Williams to create a strong music theme to characterise Bruce in the scenes where either Spielberg did not want the audience to see the shark or where the shark would not stay afloat long enough to establish its presence. The rest of the music in the film is a collection of typical sea adventure themes that have no hint of the horror theme.

Another film that achieved this memorable total integration of music and moving images is the shower murder scene in Alfred Hitchcock's *Psycho* where Bernard Herrmann's music is also chillingly linked with the shower curtain and knife.

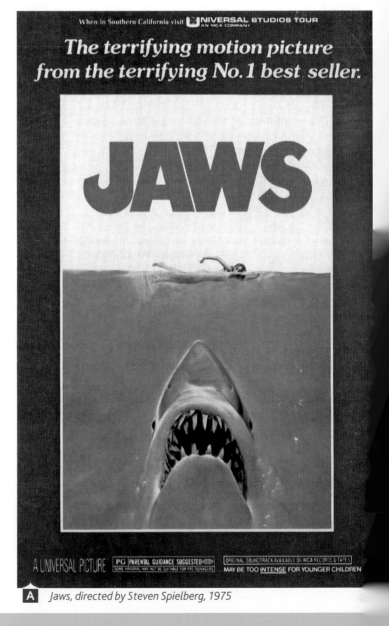

A   *Jaws, directed by Steven Spielberg, 1975*

Activity

1 Listen to the main theme and then play the beginning (using the notes E and F). You may be surprised at just how simple it is, yet it is so effective.

Analyse the importance of:

a the rhythm

b the fanfare, like three notes going up and coming down, and then

c the orchestration.

Discuss with your group how exactly the picture is painted with sound.

Stravinsky's music for the ballet *Rite of Spring* is similar in many ways to the *Jaws* score.

Your study of film music will help you in two ways:

- Firstly the old adage 'simplest is best' is evidenced in this music score. When John Williams first shared his main theme for *Jaws* with Spielberg he played it on the piano. Low in pitch, it begins with just two notes a semitone apart and Spielberg, when he first heard it quickly warmed to this musical signal that the shark was present.

- Secondly, even in professional film making with teams of experts, everything does not always go to plan (e.g. the sinking Bruce). There is often an innovative way around difficulties, and finding a solution usually necessitates creative collaboration (see Chapter 1, page 27–8). You, as an individual and as part of a group, will build a good team relationship and when things go wrong, and you get the 'Mugwumps', the creative 'zing' that you get when a solution is found will compensate for those brief moments of despair.

Activities

Look at the animation called *Creature Comforts* by Nick Park. From this series of interviews with animated characters, choose those that relate to the sea. Analyse how the audience is engaged by the conversations.

2 In your groups discuss the placement of the microphone for the interviews. It is a silly yet engaging nuance that you may or may not like.

3 Analyse the animators' use of gesture and mannerism and identify how it creates engaging communication.

3 Nick Park *animation, seagulls in conversation*

∞ links

See www. creaturecomforts.tv/ uk/ to view trailers from *Creature Comforts* by Nick Park.

Points to help you create music to use with moving images

- A successful music score is carefully cued and placed to enhance the dramatic impact.
- From the music, the audience pick up references of the visual, moving images.
- The first place you could use music or song is with the opening credits.
- The emotion or the physicality of the images can be reinforced by the music at key points.
- A **music motif** can identify characters and then be developed to communicate the changing emotion of a character.
- You could think about using **diegetic music**, **emotional impact music**, pastiche or **comic music**, and using **underscore** and **synchronisation**.

Activities

Research the grounding of the container vessel at Branscombe in January 2007.

4 Create the two storyboards for Scene 1 and 2 in Table **B** below. Plan the presentation for a group of five students.

5 Ensure that each student has a clearly defined role combining two art forms. Adjust the time plan in the left-hand column to meet your storyboard needs.

Extension activities

1 **Moving Images study suggestions**

Watch the classic Jacques Tati film *Les Vacances de M. Hulot* or the animation *Creature Comforts* by Nick Park (pay particular attention to the sea characters from the animation).

2 **Further Music study suggestions**

Listen to one of the four 'Sea Interludes' from the opera *Peter Grimes* by Benjamin Britten or *Fingal's Cave* by Mendelssohn and identify the way that rhythm, melody, instruments and pitch are used to communicate the sea.

C *The grounding planner*

Title	The Time	Director	Composer
The Shipwreck	January 2007		Fanfare original composition
			Action adventure music

Visual effects	Editor	Starring	
Group logo, props and models		Actors	

Time	The scenes	The music
0.00	The group's logo	Original fanfare theme
10	People scurrying across the shingle beach at dusk	No music, only the sound of footsteps on the shingle beach
0.25	A dark looming shadow of the beached container vessel	Introduction – mysterious, dark and menacing
0.35	Title sequence: Pale blue letters over the dark shadowy silhouette	leading into
		Action adventure music (two short melodic motifs A and B)
1.00	Scene 1 (see storyboard 1)	Motif A – developed
1.25	Scene 2 (see storyboard 2)	Motif B – developed
1.55	People scurrying across the shingle beach	No music only the sound of footsteps on the shingle beach
2.10–2.30	The credits showing in the circle of light from a Customs vehicle spotlight on the vessel	Action adventure music condensed to fit the 20-second time slot

AQA Examiner's tip

Moving Images is an art form with several component parts. It is very important to keep a detailed log of your personal contribution to the process so that your work can be clearly indentified in the presentation.

5

Innovation

You now have a clear idea about how to target a specific audience type and engage them with your presentation. There is now the added dimension of seeking 'individuality', 'quirkiness' and 'challenge'.

When new things come along in the arts there is a surge of interest, and after a while the crisp edge of innovation is smoothed and the excitement that was once there becomes the ordinary. The quality will not diminish as the work is analysed, discussed by recognised and experienced experts, and then quoted by yourselves as an influence on your work; it will simply be replaced with something newer. The arts have a knack of responding to each other, forming linking chains of innovation that weave a new style that no sooner is it identified, than it begins to unravel and morph into the next movement.

Below are four examples of Universal Themes. Research and develop ideas for each one. You have been given some study material points, but you may use your own interpretation of the theme if you wish.

Dreams

Explore the theme of dreams through the surrealist arts works that communicate to the viewer a dream-like world where although there is structure and form in the paintings, the chaos in the mind of the observer shares the artist's intention with the viewer. The scurrying ants may lead to Escher's illusionary works where ants are trapped in a möbius cycle and stairs go up as well as down.

Masks

Explore the theme of masks through any of the following: African masks, *Commedia del arte* masks, Venetian carnival masks and the modern masked ball. There is always intrigue and drama through disguise. Masks present challenges for the performing arts. The performer needs to be able to see and communicate clearly whilst wearing the mask. Creating masks that are innovative, durable and suitable for their purpose is a challenge for those offering Visual Arts.

Patterns

Circles are representative of many aspects of life, such as evolution, the solar system and sometimes confusion. The lyrics from the 1968 song 'The Windmills of Your Mind' (M. Legrand, A. Bergman and M. Bergman) create many images. Circles are used to form patterns too. You may also look at the film *The Thomas Crown Affair* to hear the song 'The Windmills of Your Mind' in the context of moving images. The interlinking circles of the Olympic logo are a successful visual interpretation of the spirit of the Olympic games and could lead to the exploration of other insignia and signifiers that use circles.

Improvisation

Here are some arts works that you may investigate to help you understand improvisation:

- The choreographer William Forsythe created 'Self Meant to Govern' where a dancer performs with a violinist using innovative Improvisation Technologies. You can see part of this work on YouTube.
- Improvisation is an important part of jazz music, and in a concerto 'the cadenza' was originally improvised.
- Jimi Hendrix's famous improvisation at Woodstock in 1969 can also be viewed on YouTube.

Revision activities

Nick Park on *Creature Comforts*

These animated interviews were popular when they were first introduced in 2003. They use unscripted voices of the public putting real-life interviews into the mouths of plasticine characters. They give their views of everyday topics, such as holidays by the sea, aliens, eating, evolution, surgery and gardening, in a diverse range of accents. Nick Park said that there was plenty more material to explore. What are your suggestions to keep ideas fresh and to reflect society's views now?

1. Where would you set your series?

2. What characters would you choose to use?

3. Who would your target audience be?

4. What would they sing, paint and dress in?

5. How would they dance, write poetry or lyrics and deliver a monologue about Expressive Arts?

A *Nick Park animation: figures communicating through facial expression and physical action*

6 Examination Presentation

Objectives

Acquire an understanding of how to use one of the set stimuli in the examination paper to create an original and engaging combined arts performance or presentation.

A *Getting started*

AQA *Examiner's tip*

Take the time to make sure you understand exactly what is required of you as an individual or with your group. Draw up a time management plan so that your preparation and response is focused and productive.

Summary of work

This is the third assessment for the Expressive Arts examination.

Your teacher will decide on the timetable for the Examination Presentation and will hand out the examination paper in good time for you to start the preliminary preparation period. The paper will contain the set stimuli for three Areas of Study – A, B and C. You will choose only one to respond to. The area you used for Wider Perspectives will be out of bounds, leaving you with a choice of two questions.

You will be allowed some preliminary preparation time (10–12 hours) to research and investigate, and do preliminary planning using a starting point from the set stimulus material. Your teacher will organise this time for you and remind you of the stimuli you can choose from.

You will then begin your strictly monitored period of **15 hours** to work on and present your response to your chosen question.

This Unit is externally set and marked. There are 80 marks – giving 40 per cent of the total marks for the whole examination.

The evidence of your work will be in the:

Presentation/Performance: Maximum 40 marks (20 per cent)

Working Processes: Maximum 40 marks (20 per cent)

On the last page of this chapter there is a detailed list of what you must do. To begin with, here are the essentials:

- Arrive at this point knowing the two arts forms you will be working with.
- Have an established process for devising your response – one that works for you or your group.
- Plan your 15 hours carefully, you cannot use running out of time as an excuse for not completing your work.
- Aim to present/perform a creative, expressive, innovative, original and engaging piece of work.
- Be prepared to keep an evidence trail of your Working Processes.

The gauntlet is thrown down. This is your challenge. Ban the 'yeah, but' and adopt the 'feel good, bring it on' attitude. Think like A Star – A*.

On the following pages are three questions adapted from the AQA Examination Presentation Paper.

6.1 From Past to Present

Set stimuli

Architecture

Photo **A** is an example of the work of the British architect Lord Norman Foster. The Millennium Bridge links the past to the present through the image. The Millennium Bridge has been described as a 'ribbon of steel' across the River Thames leading to St Paul's Cathedral. The spring collection of Gareth Pugh echoes Lord Foster's architectural elements in the dress shown.

A   *Lord Norman Foster's Millennium Bridge and the Hearst Tower echoed in a spring 2009 look from Gareth Pugh*

Further stimuli based on 'architecture':

- the recording and celebration of famous buildings through moving images, paintings and photography
- the architectural inventions of Philippe Decouflé as used in his dance works and Cirque du Soleil productions
- the 'monstrous carbuncle', reports and commentary on the extension to the National Gallery
- poetry and lyrics that relate to famous buildings such as the Taj Mahal and the Twin Towers.

Responding to stimuli A

You have a preliminary preparation period (up to 10–12 hours). Discuss your first spontaneous responses to the stimulus 'architecture' with your group and listen to the guidance that your teacher will give you. Then explore 'architecture' by researching the stimulus material. It is a good idea to keep an open mind and follow a train of thought.

For each suggestion, seek information that may have the potential to be developed further. If you are in a group it is a good idea to share this task among your group members and then discuss the outcome.

For example, the Millennium Bridge:

- Pedestrian bridge across the River Thames linking the Tate Modern on Bankside with St Paul's Cathedral.

B   *Costumes with architectural form from the work Tricodex choreographed by Philippe Decouflé*

It famously developed a tendency to sway when first opened to the public and was closed. Engineers added structural devices to make the bridge stable in use, saving the pride in British design.

Another famous bridge, the Brooklyn Bridge, developed a wave-like undulation and collapsed.

Philippe Decouflé:

Responsible for the choreography and strange architectural forms in the opening and closing ceremonies of the sixteenth Winter Olympics at Albertville (Savoie) in 1992.

He explored the possibilities of contemporary dance with choreographer Alwin Nikolais, creating shape and form through movement and innovative props.

C   *Gehry's Purple Ribbon Hotel*

The *Cirque du Soleil* show was described as clever movement, rather than dance showing life evolving. Looking at this work will expand your understanding of performers in the performance space creating shapes and forms. It is different, challenging concepts of dance, and it may spark innovative ideas for representing architectural shape and form in the performance space through Physical Theatre and Contemporary Dance.

Below are some more ideas to get you started if the research of the stimuli has not given you inspiration.

You could create an original costume and choreograph a dance that uses the line, shape and architectural form of a building. The architect Gehry uses amazing shapes in his designs and the orange Lanvin Dress from the Spring 2008 collection shows a similar flounce effect. (see Photo **C** and **D**).

Compose a piece of music that is inspired by the swaying motion of the Millennium Bridge. The music could have a calmer middle section reflecting the stabilising engineering works. Integrate the music with Visual Arts that complement the music through the CD cover design. (see Photo **C**)

D   *Lanvin dress from Spring 2008*

Create a short tourist film to show how the 'ribbon of steel' links the Globe Theatre and Tate Modern on Bankside with St Paul's Cathedral and the City. Through drama you could create characters from the past who meet those in the present communicating the history of the location.

Use the pyramid outside the Louvre to show the stark contrast between 'architecture past and present'. Create a scripted dramatic presentation of the outrage expressed about the pyramid when it was first built in the 1980s.

Activity

Create a presentation, integrating two art forms, in response to one or more of the stimuli for the topic of 'architecture'.

E   *Pyramid outside the Louvre*

6.2 Peoples and Places

■ Set stimuli

Volcanoes

The image in Photo **A** is of Pele the Hawaiian (Polynesian) goddess of the fire in volcanoes. Legend says that she has the power of destruction and that her jealous rages cause Kilauea's eruptions, sending ribbons of fiery lava down the mountainside.

Pele appears in many forms, sometimes calm and beautiful and at other times fierce and angry, destroying everything in her path just like the fire and volcanoes that she rules over. Her image is said to appear mysteriously in the clouds of steam that rise above the lava flows. When angry, she is said to hurl molten lava at her lovers and rivals, trapping them in misshapen bubbles of lava.

A more recent legend says that Pele puts a curse on anyone stealing from her home. Those who have had bad luck since taking rocks away as souvenirs send pieces of lava rock back to Hawaii, hoping to release the curse.

Here are some further stimuli based on 'volcanoes':

- The traditional arts works of Kamchatka in the far east of Russia. There are distinct groups of people who call this fiery yet beautiful land home. This area is part of the Ring of Fire and it has the highest density of volcanoes and associated volcanic activity in the world.

- The 13th-century Icelandic myths about volcanoes were made into a television drama with song called *Volcano Saga*. It tells the story of a young woman whose dreams foretell the future.

- The dramatic eye-witness account of the eruption of Mount Vesuvius in AD 79 and the destruction of Pompeii as told through the writings of Pliny the Younger.

- Volcano songs: active volcanoes produce low-frequency sounds, acoustic signals, that can be described as songs. Volcanoes give those listening a warning that they may erupt, unlike earthquakes, which give few warning signs before they strike.

Objectives

Explore Peoples and Places through 'volcanoes' and develop ideas that can be used to create a presentation integrating two art forms.

Write a clear aim for your work and target a specific audience.

Activity

1. Create a presentation, integrating two art forms, in response to one or more of the stimuli for the topic of 'volcanoes'.

A *Pele, the goddess of the fire in volcanoes*

Responding to stimuli **B**

By responding to these examples of stimulus material, you are learning how to develop ideas through chosen art forms and by exploring combined arts outcomes.

At this point, it is a good time to remind you of the importance of having a very clear aim for your work and a specific target audience.

Remember that you will only answer one question for the actual examination and the question you respond to must be a different area of study to the one submitted for Controlled Assessment. You will have two left to choose from.

B   *Pompeii, a Roman town half destroyed and buried during the erruption of Mount Vesuvius*

Activity

2   Below are some ideas relating to the given stimuli. Discuss each one with a partner and then express each idea as an aim. This will help you to understand and apply a clear pathway to achieving.

For example, the group decide they want to: 'Tell the story of what happened to a tourist who stole a piece of lava from Pele. They took the lava home as a souvenir of their Hawaiian holiday not realising that Pele puts a curse on those who steal from her home.'

The aim for this work could be: 'Using Drama, Music and Original Writing our aim is to engage an adult audience in a 'who done it' type mystery about a jinx that seems to be creating havoc with a family's life since they returned from holiday in Hawaii.'

Now write your own aims for these three suggestions:

a   Using Visual Arts and Music, create an original soundtrack to complement your art work where you show Pele's two sides – the beautiful and gentle, contrasting with the fiery, tempestuous and destructive.

b   Manipulate original footage of volcanic eruptions and lava flows from the Ring of Fire and use this as a back projection for Dance, Drama or Original Writing that communicates the contrast of the flowing fluidity of molten lava with the dynamic, convulsive eruption of volcanoes.

c   Create a dance drama where the frozen images of Pele's rivals are released. Once free, they tell the story of how they came to be trapped as misshapen pillars of rock. Pele is furious at their release and there is an outrageous and dynamic ending.

Extension activity

In AD 79 a fleet of Roman ships under the command of Pliny the Elder were stationed at Misenum. When Mount Vesuvius began to erupt they sailed across the Bay of Naples to attempt a rescue.

a   Research this event and plan a response using your chosen art forms.

b   State a clear aim.

c   Organise your ideas into five episodes. You may wish to consider distorting the time line.

d   Review the potential of the five episodes to show a range of pace and dynamic in the delivery of the performance.

6.3   Universal themes

Set stimuli

Shadows

The stimuli based on the topic of 'shadows' are:

- Silhouette cutting as established in 18th century Paris. A street activity that could be considered a performance art using shadows.
- *Peter Pan*: Chapter 2 – The Shadow. Mrs Darling neatly rolls up the lost shadow and places it in a drawer for safe keeping.
- Trisha Brown in 'If You Couldn't See Me'. Performed with the dancers, back to the audience, as if dancing with the shadow at the back of the stage.
- Tim Noble and Sue Webster. *Dirty White Trash (with Gulls)*, 1998. This image shows six months' worth of artists' trash carefully arranged so that when a light projector is used the trash can cast the shadow of two figures.

Responding to stimuli C

You are now familiar with the method of working – 10–12 hours for Preliminary Preparation and then the timed 15-hour section to create and present your work.

You could:

- Through Moving Images explore shadows that communicate what was once, compared to the reality of what is now. Using drama develop a narrative placing the mysterious shadows in constantly changing contexts of then and now.
- Using dance and drama, release the shadow from the drawer where Mrs Darling has neatly rolled it up and placed it for safekeeping. What happens next is beyond belief.
- Write a song, music and lyrics about a person who you watch dancing, but you cannot see their face as they never turn around. Use side lighting to cast a shadow of the figure dancing to the song. A face to be revealed at the end through a reflection in a mirror at the back of the performance space.
- Create a presentation called 'Mistaken for Reality' taking inspiration from the Tim Noble and Sue Webster art work. Shadows come and go according to the light source that is shining on objects or people. This can make them appear mysterious, threatening or even decadent, as in the stimulus Photo **A**.

> ## Objectives
>
> Explore the Universal Theme 'shadows' to develop ideas that can be used to create a presentation integrating two art forms.

> ## Activity
>
> 1. Create a presentation, integrating two art forms, in response to one or more of the stimuli for the topic of 'shadows'.

A   *In this image a figure walks out of a tunnel surrounded by shadows of steamy words that make no sense. Was there an argument that he is walking away from?*

B *Here is an example of a student's Visual Arts response to the theme 'shadows'. The image will be projected and become part of a series of backdrops for a dramatic presentation called 'Would you like a coffee?'*

Shadow puppetry is an art form in it own right, but consider how you can use a series of shadow images to communicate narrative.

In horror films it is often the shadowy image that is the most scary because it is not always entirely clear what it is and therefore it is open to the interpretation of the audience. Explore and film shadowy images.

Watch the song 'Money, Money' from the musical *Cabaret* (the film version directed and choreographed by Bob Fosse). Joel Grey as Master of Ceremonies and Liza Minnelli as Sally Bowles move behind a screen and dance in silhouette. Discuss how effective you think this is and find other examples of a similar use of silhouettes.

Activities

2   See how many suggestions your group can make to progress the theme 'Shadows' beyond a simple response. Identify the best idea by choosing the one that will enable you to achieve marks in the higher mark bands. You will need to develop innovative ideas that use a high degree of precision and control in the skills and techniques of your chosen art forms in ways that are inspired, original and sophisticated. Has this idea the potential to become a highly sophisticated and successful presentation?

3   Take the group's best idea and apply the process established in Chapter 1 (see 'Developing ideas' and 'Away of working', pages 22–3 and 27–8).

4   Develop and shape the idea. Identify processes and techniques to use for your two chosen art forms.

5   Explore, select and apply appropriate processes and techniques to move the work on. Know why they are appropriate. Review, modify and refine the work ensuring that you relate to the stimulus material, the aim and the target audience.

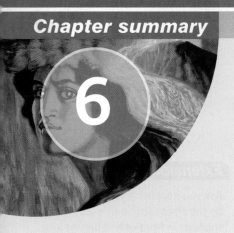
Conclusion

You should now be feeling confident about the Examination Presentation. Here are the reminders as promised.

You will:

✔ Respond to *one* or more of the set stimuli and, either working alone or in a group, create and present an *original* response that combines and integrates the chosen art forms.

✔ Prior to the examination use the permitted time to research and investigate the stimuli, and do preliminary planning and then use the maximum of *15 hours* for the preparation and completion of your piece.

✔ Apply skills, processes and techniques; shape and structure your ideas; review, modify and refine the work as it progresses.

✔ Keep a clear *evidence trail* for your Working Processes submission, detailing the progress of your work and the contributions you made.

✔ Provide evidence of the development of ideas for *both art forms*, showing the ways they will be woven together to compliment and support each other.

✔ On the record sheet provided for you, identify the two art forms you want to be assessed on and list all of the items included in your Working Processes evidence.

✔ If you are doing a performance, consider carefully an approximate length. Some combinations of art forms, for example combinations including Dance, require shorter times; some longer, for example, combinations including Drama. As an absolute maximum it must be longer than 15 minutes. If there are fewer than five in the group the presentation will be proportionally shorter.

✔ Be very clear that you must do all of this work under *teacher supervision* and *receive no help*.

The three stages of the Examination Presentation are as follows:

1 Investigating and planning: the time allowed for you to explore the stimuli is 10–12 hours.

2 Your practical work begins and this is supervised and monitored by your teacher, ensuring that the work is your own or if you are working in a group your contribution can be identified. You must keep evidence of the development of your work for your Working Processes submission.

3 Presenting or performing your work: feel good and proud of your sophisticated and successfu combined arts work.

Fifteen hours – hey, that's months!

A *Use your time wisely*

Glossary

A

Absent fathers: where the father is not actively involved with raising his child.

Advertising: the description or presentation of a product, idea or organisation, disseminated through such media as television, radio, newspapers, posters, mailings and the internet, in order to induce individuals to buy, support or approve of it.

Alliteration: formed by a number of adjacent or closely related words starting with the same letter or sound.

Anacrusic: not starting on the first beat of the bar.

Analyse: break a dance sequence into its movement component parts such as walk, turn, twist.

Assassination: the surprise murder of a person, often in public.

Assonance: an imperfect rhyme formed by two or more adjacent or closely related words having the same stressed vowels but not the same consonants, or the same consonants but not the same vowels.

Audio dub: to add audio tracks during editing.

B

Biopic: a biographical, and often dramatic, film or television programme about an individual.

C

Call and response: a style of performing where one person or a group calls a statement or question and another person or group responds with a reply or an answer. Spiritual and work songs use this style.

Camcorder: a video camera that enables you to record on tape, DVD or memory card.

Choreographic devices: the tools to help you create a successful dance such as the use of repetition of motifs and phrases of movement in appropriate places of your dance.

Chroma-key: a function for combining two images where one colour in a layer is made transparent. A plain blue or green background is used, so revealing the image behind. In television and film it is called 'blue screen'. This process can be used to superimpose a real character onto another image such as a background location.

Colour-pass: used in the editing stage to allow a single colour to show through an otherwise mono-chrome image.

Comic music: music that closely follows the dramatic action, such as a descending glissando for falling down, or using a muted trumpet for laughter or pizzicato strings for creeping up on someone.

Construction: the way the sections of the work are brought together.

Contemporary: belonging to the world as we live in it now, whether it is our home or school community, the society of our own country or a society in another part of the world.

Counterpoint (contrapuntal): two contrasting compositional elements used at the same time to create tension or heightened effect.

CU: close-up. Camera shot with the detail of the subject filling the screen.

Cultures: the attitudes and values that inform a society.

Cuts: changes from one image to another.

D

Diegetic music: the music that is part of the action in the scene. For example, the band playing in the park, or the rehearsal music in a dance studio, or the music from a car radio.

Docu-drama: a documentary-style programme with dramatic re-enactments of the principal characters and events.

Double entendre: a word or phrase with two meanings.

E

Emotional impact music: the music that heightens the emotional state of the characters.

Engage: draw your audience into your performance/presentation.

Episodic: divided into episodes that may or may not follow a time line or narrative.

Exploration improvisations: drama techniques to 'find out' something about a character or situation.

F

Flair: an exceptional talent, a perceptive and stylish application of a skill.

Focus: sharpness and clarity of the image.

Forms: fixed styles of artistic organisation. Music gives us some names of structural patterns such as Binary: A: B; Ternary: A: B: A; Rondo: A: B: A: C: A: D etc.; Variation: A: A1: A2: A3.

G

Genre: a type or style of presentation.

Graphics: title and credit sequences and other illustrations such as graphs or charts.

I

Images: the component parts of an arts work which stimulate responses in the imagination of an audience.

Imaginative: showing a high degree of imagination to make up, create or devise a response to the task set.

Improvising: simultaneously creating and performing movements without preplanning. Reacting to an idea without first thinking about it.

Innovative: new, unexpected and quite different.

Issue: an important subject for discussion.

L

LS: long shot. Camera shot which includes the subject and the location.

M

Manipulative: a way of handling or managing events or people so that they do what you want them to.

Method: a series of actions that you learn or that you establish. They will help you to progress your work.

Metrical structure: the rhythm of a line, or a sequence of lines, of poetry made up of stressed and unstressed syllables. This too sometimes becomes a pattern which is repeated throughout the poem.

Monochrome: black and white.

Motifs: simple movements or short movement phrases that represent the important characteristics of the whole dance.

Motivation: the thoughts and feelings that a character must have to act in the way they do. An actor must reconstruct the motivation of a character to make the action convincing.

Music motif: a short piece of music to identify a particular location, character, scene or event.

N

Narrative: the telling of a story or sequence of events.

Nuclear family: a mother, father and their children.

O

Ostinato: a continually repeated musical phrase or rhythm.

P

Pack-shot: image of the product in its packaging so that it can be recognised in the store.

Piggy-backing: using elements of a previously advertised and popular product to help advertise your own product, e.g. a successful pop song as the backing track for your advertisement.

R

Realism: art which depicts reality without any emotional interpretation or flamboyance.

Reinforcement: repeated references to the product in the advertisement, either visually or aurally.

Rhyme scheme: when words with the same or similar sounds at the end occur, such as row/blow. The scheme is the structure used in the poem to create rhyme.

Rhymes: two words rhyme when they have the same sound in their last syllable/syllables. The sound may be just a vowel or a combination of consonants and vowels.

S

Shooting script: the order in which your shots will be filmed on location.

Signifiers: specific, identifiable elements that can be clearly associated with something, e.g. the Louis Vuitton monogram and luggage.

Soundscape: painting a picture using sounds to set the mood and atmosphere of a specific location and time.

Stanza: the verse of a poem. A stanza works in the same way as a paragraph in prose and is a structural unit in the composition of a poem – often establishing a pattern which is repeated throughout the poem.

Stereotype: a person or thing that conforms to an unjustifiable mental picture.

Storyboard: a visual representation of your programme to help you visualise a shot and see it in relation to the rest of the programme.

Strategy: a plan to help you do the required work.

Structure: a framework that brings your ideas together. This may be an existing organisational pattern or it may be a unique structure specific to the needs of the presentation/ performance.

Study: the analysis and exploration of the works chosen to broaden your understanding of communicating through the arts.

Synchronisation: matching of the sound and the shots.

T

Target audience: the identity of the precise type of audience, used to inform the planning and style of your work.

Target group: the specific group that the advertisement is aimed at.

The Mugwumps: a made up, non-technical term for the way you feel when nothing seems to be working.

Traditions: tales, beliefs and practices passed from generation to generation and belonging to a specific family, people or culture.

Transitions: mixes or special effects between images.

Types of shot: establishing shots, medium shots, close-ups, etc.

U

Underscore: the background music used under the dialogue.

V

Visual imagery: when a writer uses words to create images in the reader's mind to inspire the reader's imagination to evoke a personal response.

W

Word painting: using the pitch of the notes to enhance the meaning of the words, e.g. 'What does this mean to me?' (the melody to rise at the end of the question because the natural inflection of the voice is to rise).

Index